Traits of Good Writing

4–5

Written by
Mary Murray

Editor: Carla Hamaguchi
Illustrator: Jenny Campbell
Designer/Production: Moonhee Pak/Cari Helstrom
Cover Designer: Barbara Peterson
Art Director: Tom Cochrane
Project Director: Carolea Williams

Table of Contents

Introduction

Each book in the *Power Practice*™ series contains dozens of ready-to-use activity pages to provide students with skill practice. Use the fun activities to supplement and enhance what you are already teaching in your classroom. Give an activity page to students as independent class work, or send the pages home as homework to reinforce skills taught in class. An answer key is included at the end of each book to provide verification of student responses.

The activity pages in *Traits of Good Writing 4–5* provide an ideal way to enhance students' writing skills. The book features activities that target six important traits of writing: Ideas and Content, Organization, Voice, Word Choice, Sentence Fluency, and Conventions. These fun and challenging activities give students many opportunities to practice each writing skill in a meaningful way.

As students learn to recognize the traits of good writing, they will brainstorm and develop topics, develop and organize their thoughts and ideas, and then put their writing skills into practice. Students will gain confidence in their writing ability as they enhance grammar and usage skills and gain an awareness of how word choice and sentence development influence their writing. As your young authors establish a style and voice of their own, they will be well on their way to becoming successful and competent writers.

Use these ready-to-go activities to "recharge" skill review and give students the power to succeed!

Name _____ Date _____

What Do You Know?

BRAINSTORMING TOPICS

A good writer will write about what he or she knows. Think of some things you know a lot about. What are your talents? What do you enjoy doing? You may know a lot about a person, a sport, a pet, a place, a hobby or game, or some kind of food. Look at this list of ideas. Circle the ideas you could write about. Add your own ideas in the blank spaces.

baseball	making cookies	a great book	soccer	a favorite movie
my dad	our family	a family vacation	my pet	riding a bike
camping	painting	my bedroom	your city	my mom
a favorite teacher	my house	doing chores	ice cream	pizza

 Which three topics would be easiest for you to write about? Draw a star by these. Write about one of these topics.

Picture Perfect

GATHERING IDEAS

You can get ideas for writing by looking at pictures. Look at each picture and read each sentence. Write the letter of the sentence that corresponds with each picture.

1

2

3

4

5

6

a. Who will make the first splash, the squirrel or the finch?

b. Planting, digging, weeding, and watering are important tasks for the committed gardener.

c. My shoe stuck to the newly tarred road. I didn't know what to do, so I just ran.

d. It isn't easy giving Rex a bath. I usually end up getting wetter than he.

e. When Jason found a twenty-dollar bill on the sidewalk, he dropped his backpack and ran home to tell his mom.

f. The floodwater was so high that animals would do anything to find a dry place to perch.

Traits of Good Writing • 4–5 © 2004 Creative Teaching Press

Name _____ Date _____

Experiences
BRAINSTORMING IDEAS

Experiences give you ideas for writing. What interesting experiences have you had? Look at the list of experiences on this page. Circle each experience you have had.

having fun at a water park	sledding down a big hill
getting stung by a bee	riding a skateboard
getting along with brothers and sisters	feelings you have when a pet dies
playing baseball	catching frogs and other creatures
building a robot	being a good friend
breaking an arm or leg	ice-skating
making a submarine sandwich	a fun family picnic
mixing up a batch of great cookies	entertaining yourself on a long car ride
riding a city bus	planting a garden
getting stitches	building a tree fort
in-line skating	making a bed
fishing from shore	planting a tree
having a cavity filled	setting up a lemonade stand
what it's like to be the new kid at school	collecting football or baseball cards
getting good grades at school	playing an instrument
wearing braces	planning a neighborhood circus
washing a car	cleaning the garage
taking care of a younger sibling	moving to a new house
water-skiing	a day at the carnival

Think of six more experiences you have had that you could write about. Write them in the blank spaces.

_____   _____

_____   _____

_____   _____

Now choose an experience and write all you can about that experience.

Traits of Good Writing • 4–5 © 2004 Creative Teaching Press

Name _____ Date _____

Let's Explore!

Observing and Gathering Details

Exploring and observing are important skills to use when writing. When you observe your surroundings you can gather many details to use in your writing.

Go outside or to another location and observe your surroundings. Write your observations in the chart. Use your five senses to help you discover specific details. Write any interesting or important facts about the items that you observe.

What I	Interesting	Important
saw:		
heard:		
smelled:		
felt:		
tasted:		

 Use the information you gathered to write a paragraph about your observations.

Traits of Good Writing • 4–5 © 2004 Creative Teaching Press

Project Pet

Grouping Ideas or Details

Organizing ideas and details before you begin writing is important. Look at the information inside the box. Write each detail in the appropriate section of the graphic organizer.

Brush her fur	Carrots	Hold and hug her	Pellets
Squeaks and chatters	Chews on chew stick	Apple slices	Sleeps
Give her food and water	Bathe once a week	Clean her cage	Hay
Take her for a walk	Build a maze for her	Clip her nails	Grass

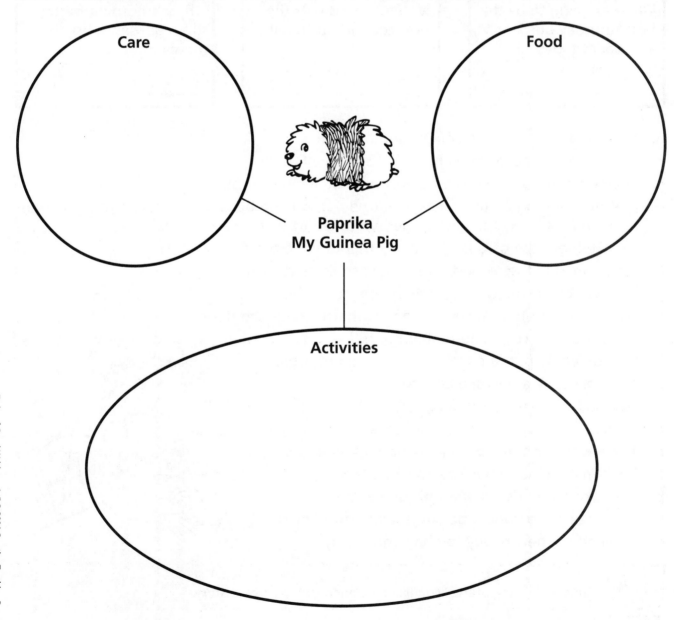

Care

Food

Paprika
My Guinea Pig

Activities

Start a Story

STORY STARTERS

A **story starter** helps you get an idea for writing. Look at each of these story starters. Then read the details below. Write the letters of the details that match each story starter.

It was a crazy day in art class. _____ _____ _____	It was the best birthday surprise I ever had. _____ _____ _____	I never had so much fun on a rainy day. _____ _____ _____
This was going to be the best Saturday our family ever spent together. _____ _____ _____	My mom is usually the best cook in our family. _____ _____ _____	There's nothing better than getting a brand-new pet. _____ _____ _____

a. My grandma came up from Chicago to see me.

b. Ricky opened the jar of paint, and it spilled all over.

c. I named him Clyde and vowed he would be my best friend.

d. I set my painting on the windowsill to dry. The wind blew in and my painting landed on Jennifer's back. The back of her white T-shirt was covered in paint.

e. I walked into the garage and all my friends were there.

f. We jumped in the biggest puddles we could find.

g. He loves to see me when I come home from school.

h. Mrs. Hagen dropped a clay pot and it shattered on the floor.

i. We put on raincoats and rubber boots.

j. She somehow put salt in the cake instead of sugar.

k. Mom gave me a new skateboard.

l. Dad had the van packed for a day at the beach.

m. Afterwards, we collected 36 night crawlers for fishing.

n. There was a ton of frosting piled on a salty cake.

o. Mom made huge submarine sandwiches.

p. The cake didn't rise. It was only one inch high.

q. The pizza parlor would be our last stop for dinner.

r. I trained my new puppy to obey right away.

 Choose the story starter you like best and write your own story.

Traits of Good Writing • 4–5 © 2004 Creative Teaching Press

It's Time to Write

WRITING PROMPTS

> A writing prompt can help you think of ideas to write about.
> Writing that shares information or explains something is called **expository writing**.
> Writing that tells a story is called **narrative writing**.

Read each writing prompt. Shade in the circle next to the letter **E** if it is an expository writing prompt. Shade in the circle next to the letter **N** if it is a narrative writing prompt.

1 E ○ N ○   Explain how to make a root beer float.

2 E ○ N ○   Write about a spaceship that landed on your school playground.

3 E ○ N ○   Tell how to get to your house from school.

4 E ○ N ○   Write a letter to your parents explaining why you're old enough to sleep over at a friend's house.

5 E ○ N ○   Tell what happened on your last family vacation.

6 E ○ N ○   Explain the likenesses and differences between kickball and soccer.

7 E ○ N ○   Tell about a frightening experience that you and a friend had together.

8 E ○ N ○   Gather information about porcupines and write what you learn.

9 E ○ N ○   Write about the worst day you've ever had.

10 E ○ N ○   Tell your reasons why participating in sports is good for kids.

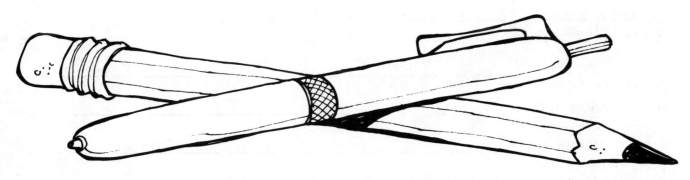

Please Expand

ELABORATE ON IDEAS

Simple sentences can be expanded to create more elaborate and **detailed sentences.**

Example: simple sentence	—The cat purred.
add "when"	—Last night, the cat purred.
add "size"	—Last night, the petite cat purred.
name a place	—Last night, the petite cat purred outside my front door.
add a name	—Last night, Carolyn's petite cat purred outside my front door.

Expand each simple sentence.

1 The dog barked.

When: _____

Size or Color: _____

Place: _____

Name: _____

2 The man ate.

When: _____

Size or Color: _____

Place: _____

Name: _____

3 The team played.

When: _____

Size or Color: _____

Place: _____

Name: _____

Traits of Good Writing • 4–5 © 2004 Creative Teaching Press

Name _____ Date _____

What's the Topic?

TOPIC SENTENCES

A **topic sentence** is the first sentence in the paragraph that tells what the paragraph is about. Read each set of sentences. Circle the topic sentence.

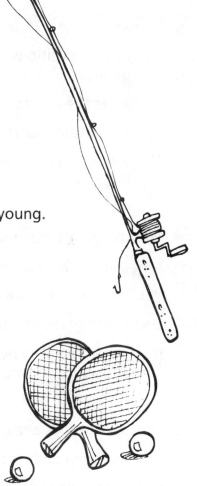

1 Puppies like to play.
A puppy makes a wonderful pet.
It's fun to take a puppy on a walk.

2 We always catch a lot of fish.
Fishing with a fishing guide is the best way to fish.
He teaches me which bait to use to catch the best fish.

3 The teachers are nice and recess is fun.
You learn a lot about different things.
School is great!

4 My grandpa is a great guy.
He always jokes around with me and makes me laugh.
Grandpa tells me interesting stories about when he was young.

5 They wash their food before they eat it.
Raccoons will eat almost anything.
Raccoons are interesting animals.

6 It's fun to play with two or four players.
Ping-Pong™ is a great game.
It takes talent to keep bouncing the ball on the table.

7 The players are very talented.
It's always fun to see who wins.
Watching a professional basketball game is exciting.

Write a topic sentence for this unfinished paragraph.

_____

There are so many different animals to see. You can buy a souvenir and a snack at the concession stand. On Sundays you can take a ride on a camel or help the zookeeper feed the tortoises. Mom says the zoo is a great place for fun family time.

Traits of Good Writing • 4–5 © 2004 Creative Teaching Press

Parts of a Paragraph

PARAGRAPHING

> A **paragraph** has three main parts: the topic sentence, the supporting details, and the conclusion.
> The first sentence of a paragraph is always indented.
> The **topic sentence** tells what the paragraph is about.
> The **details** tell more about the topic.
> The **concluding sentence** restates the topic or reminds the reader what the paragraph was about.

Look at each set of sentences. Write **topic**, **detail**, or **concluding** to identify each sentence.

1 Everyone plays a different position. _____

The various positions are defender, midfielder, forward, and goalie. _____

They pass the ball to each other and hope to score a goal. _____

Soccer is a team sport. _____

The players on a soccer team need to work together to win the game. _____

2 You change its shavings once a week. _____

A hamster is an ideal pet for a busy fifth grader. _____

You only need to give it food and water once a day. _____

Every fifth grader should have a hamster for a pet. _____

It's a cute animal to hold and pet, but when you're busy it's happy without you. _____

3 Call your friends ahead of time to meet you at the pool. _____

Bring a towel and be sure to put on lots of sunscreen. _____

Spending a day at the pool is great summer fun. _____

Pack a lunch for when you're hungry. _____

The best way to spend a summer day is with your friends at the pool. _____

 Write a topic sentence, three supporting details, and a concluding sentence for a topic of your choice.

Sports

COMPARE AND CONTRAST

It's important to organize ideas and information when comparing and contrasting two things. You can organize information by how things are alike and how they are different using a Venn diagram.

Fill in the Venn diagram with the words from the box. Add some of your own ideas as well.

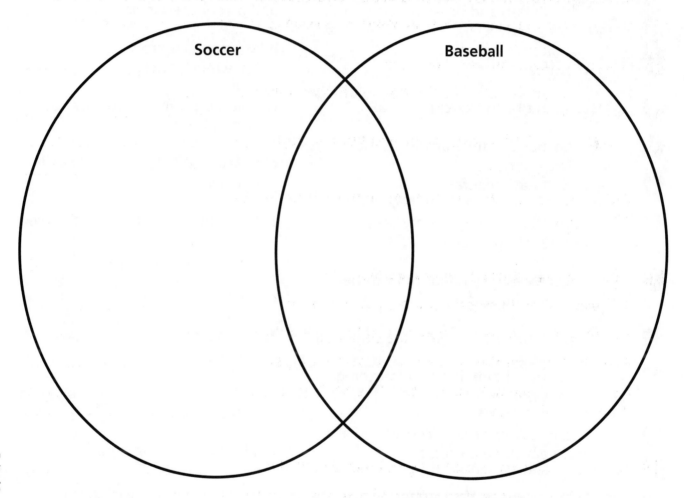

Soccer   Baseball

play with one ball	wear a uniform	use a glove	use a bat
kick the ball	catch the ball	wear spikes	has a goalie
can't touch the ball	throw the ball	small ball	big ball
wear a cap	wear a batting glove	uses an umpire	many players on a team

Draw a Venn diagram. Choose two topics you could compare and contrast.

Name _____ Date _____

Healthy Me

CAUSE AND EFFECT

Cause and effect writing explains why certain things happen. For example, if you only eat candy for dinner, lunch, and breakfast, you will not feel well.

Read each statement. Match each cause to its effect.

1 _____ I don't wash and brush my hair.

2 _____ I drink soda instead of milk all the time.

3 _____ I haven't been exercising at all.

4 _____ I stay up too late watching a movie.

5 _____ I don't eat breakfast.

6 _____ I don't brush and floss my teeth before going to bed.

7 _____ I never wash my hands during the cold and flu season.

8 _____ I spend too much time at the computer.

9 _____ I eat lots of junk food and nothing that is healthy.

10 _____ Mom makes the best chocolate cake, but I eat three pieces.

a. I'm very tired in school.

b. My stomach growls and I don't have much energy.

c. I won't get my calcium or have strong bones.

d. I wasn't able to run very fast in gym class.

e. I had the worst stomachache ever.

f. I have two cavities. Yikes!

g. I will likely catch a cold or flu.

h. I won't have much time for outdoor play.

i. I will be weak and probably gain extra weight.

j. I'll have dirty, ratty hair.

Write a cause and effect paragraph about being healthy. Use some of the information from above in your paragraph.

_____

_____

_____

_____

Traits of Good Writing • 4–5 © 2004 Creative Teaching Press

Name _____ Date _____

Fishbowl

SEQUENCING INSTRUCTIONS

Read the instructions for cleaning a fishbowl. Put the steps in the correct order by numbering them from 1 to 10. Notice how the writer uses the words **first**, **next**, **then**, **after**, and **finally**.

1 _____ Finally, put the fish into the clean fishbowl.

2 _____ Then add warm water.

3 _____ Place a drop of dish liquid in the dirty bowl.

4 _____ Be careful not to let the pebbles fall into the drain.

5 _____ First, pour the fish and some of the water into a different container.

6 _____ Let the fresh water stand until it's room temperature.

7 _____ Then pour the rest of the dirty water down the drain.

8 _____ After that, rinse everything several times until no more soap bubbles appear.

9 _____ Next, wash and scrub the inside of the bowl, along with any shells, coral, or rocks with the soapy water.

10 _____ Then add fresh water to the clean bowl.

Write instructions for how to do one of the following: make an ice-cream sundae, make your bed, or clean your room. Be sure to use "order words" (first, next, after that, then, finally) so that your instructions are easy to understand.

_____

_____

_____

_____

_____

_____

_____

Name _____ Date _____

In the Kitchen

SEQUENCING INSTRUCTIONS

When writing instructions, good writers sequence their steps so they are clear and easy to follow. There are two sets of instructions: one for baking a frozen pizza and another for making macaroni and cheese. The instructions are mixed up and need to be sorted. Write them in order beneath the correct heading, so the directions are easy to follow.

Cut into slices and enjoy
Pour noodles into a pan of boiling water
Stir until well combined
Place pizza in the oven
Add butter, milk, and cheese sauce packet
Unwrap pizza

Spoon into bowls and enjoy
Drain noodles
Bake for 15 minutes
Boil noodles for 7 minutes
Preheat oven to 400°
Remove pizza from the oven

Pizza

_____

_____

_____

_____

_____

_____

Macaroni and Cheese

_____

_____

_____

_____

_____

_____

Name _____ Date _____

Fun in the Sun

DETAILS AND MAIN IDEA

Read each sentence and determine if it's a main idea, detail, or irrelevant to the topic. Label each sentence with **main idea**, **detail**, or **irrelevant**.

Hiking

1. It's important to wear good shoes when you go. _____

2. Hiking is a great sport for people of all ages. _____

3. There are many parks and nature trails to choose from. _____

4. You can go hiking with family or friends. _____

5. We're having cheeseburgers for supper tonight. _____

6. It's a good idea to bring a water bottle and a pair of binoculars. _____

7. Hiking is good exercise. _____

8. Some hiking trails have steep rock stairways to climb. _____

The Water Park

1. You get lots of exercise climbing up and down all the stairs and ladders. _____

2. You can relax on inner tubes at the Lazy River. _____

3. It's important to wear sunscreen if you stay all day. _____

4. A trip to the water park is great summer fun. _____

5. It doesn't cost that much to get into the park. _____

6. You can choose from a variety of slides and rides. _____

7. My favorite song is "The Star-Spangled Banner." _____

8. Some water parks offer miniature golf and bumper cars, too. _____

9. Many people like the Wave Pool the best. _____

Think of another "fun in the sun" topic. Write a main idea and two details for the topic.

Traits of Good Writing • 4–5 © 2004 Creative Teaching Press

Name _____ Date _____

A Trip to the Library

SUPPORTING DETAILS

Read each sentence. Write **yes** by the sentences that include details you would add to a story about your trip to the library. Remember to only include details that are important, are interesting, and share information. Do not include details the reader already knows. Write **no** by the details you would not include.

1. Chloe, Allison, and I rode our bikes to the library. _____

2. The library has a green sign. _____

3. Chloe was determined to find a book on horses. _____

4. A library is a place where you get books. _____

5. Allison spent a half hour using the computer. _____

6. Chloe goes to piano lessons tomorrow. _____

7. I can't wait for supper because we're having pizza. _____

8. I found two books to help with my report on farming. _____

9. The librarian wore gold earrings. _____

10. There are many books arranged in neat rows. _____

11. We talked with our gym teacher, who was checking out videos. _____

12. The bathroom has pink curtains. _____

13. The books are all on shelves. _____

14. At checkout time, I couldn't find my library card. _____

15. My Uncle Bob works in a bookstore. _____

16. Chloe found my card on the bathroom floor. _____

17. My friends and I enjoy going to the library. _____

18. We want to start a book club. _____

19. The carpet was dirty. _____

20. The librarian said, "I'm glad you girls like to read," as she checked out our books. _____

Story Parts

Beginning, Middle, End

Every story has a beginning, a middle, and an end.
The beginning of a story tells who, what, and where. It introduces a problem.
The middle of a story tells what happens.
The end of the story tells how the problem or conflict was resolved.

Read the statements. Determine if each statement would work best as a beginning, middle, or end of a story. Write **B** if the sentence would make a good beginning, **M** for middle, or **E** for end.

1 _____ She stepped into the room and turned on the lights.

2 _____ Finally, Marcie understood why Gena wasn't very kind to others, and she was determined to be the best friend that she could be.

3 _____ Everyone gathered together to cheer the team on.

4 _____ Zach was twelve years old and five foot seven; the tallest kid in fifth grade.

5 _____ Sophie joyfully picked up her dog and held him tight as she promised, "I'm never letting you off your leash again."

6 _____ Mr. Carlyle was a short, round, cheerful man, and he'd been the town mayor for three years.

7 _____ The two of them ran through the forest as fast as they could.

8 _____ The whole gang agreed that it had been the most fun they'd ever had.

9 _____ It all began when Sheila set her backpack on the hallway floor, and Tiffany tripped over it, and everyone laughed.

10 _____ Joe and Kevin shook hands and decided they were actually glad the accident had happened, or they would have never met and become fast friends.

11 _____ Mary got up early and was ready to begin the day she had been waiting for, for so long.

12 _____ Jeremy's dad was glad he was home safe, but he still gave Jeremy a stern warning as Jeremy drifted off into a deep sleep.

13 _____ Chelsea was a quiet girl who lived in a little white house on the edge of town, near the river.

14 _____ Now Janet knew she had found a friend who was true-to-the-heart-forever.

Name _____ Date _____

Life Story

STORY WEB

Bobby wants to write a story about his life. He brainstormed many ideas but needs help organizing the information. Write each idea in the correct part of the story web.

Won the fifty-yard freestyle race	Hit a home run in a little league game
Caught a 6-inch Walleye Pike	Mrs. Jones was my third grade teacher.
Joined the Cub Scouts	I got my first A in math class.
Made many new friends	Visited the museum for a field trip
We moved from Alabama to Wisconsin.	My dad bought a new puppy.
Vacationed in California	My baby brother, Jake, was born.

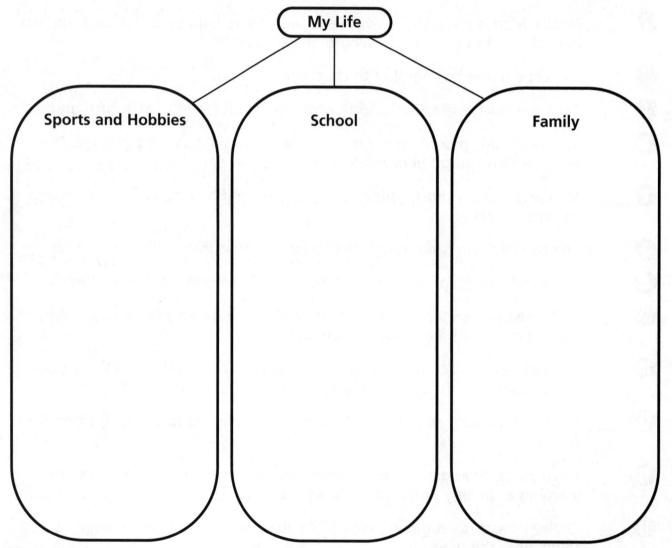

My Life

Sports and Hobbies

School

Family

Create a story web with information about your life. Then write a story and read it to a friend or family member.

Traits of Good Writing • 4–5 © 2004 Creative Teaching Press

Name _____ Date _____

A Can of Critters

ANALYZING PARTS OF A STORY

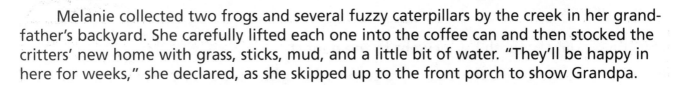

Read the story and answer each question.

Melanie collected two frogs and several fuzzy caterpillars by the creek in her grand-father's backyard. She carefully lifted each one into the coffee can and then stocked the critters' new home with grass, sticks, mud, and a little bit of water. "They'll be happy in here for weeks," she declared, as she skipped up to the front porch to show Grandpa.

Just then Melanie's mother pulled into the driveway. "Thanks for the great weekend, Grandpa," Melanie said, as she hugged her grandfather goodbye. On the ride home, she told her mother all about the fun weekend she had, except for the critters in the can in the back seat. Melanie knew her mother wouldn't approve, so she planned to sneak them into her bedroom as soon as they got home.

Melanie said "hi" to her dad and little brother and then went to her bedroom to unpack her things. She strategically placed the can of critters behind her desk chair, hoping that her mother wouldn't find it. Melanie enjoyed an evening with her family and later on bid her new pets good night, as she fell fast asleep.

The following morning Melanie was startled awake by her mother's crackling voice, "Melanie Elizabeth Murray! What is going on in here?" she asked. "Oh, oh," Melanie thought, as she sat up in bed, "they got out." Melanie looked across the room to see two frogs perched on her desk and four of the five caterpillars crawling around the room. Melanie quickly gathered her pets together, apologized to her mom, and cleaned up the mess. Her mother watched in silence with her hands on her hips, and then sputtered, "I'll talk to you downstairs." "What a way to start the day," Melanie sighed, as she headed out to the back door to let the pets go and then quickly find her mom.

Who is the main character? _____

What is the setting? _____

How does the story begin? _____

What is the problem/conflict? _____

What happens? _____

How does the story end? _____

What is the most important moment in the story? _____

_____

Traits of Good Writing • 4–5 © 2004 Creative Teaching Press

Name _____ Date _____

Attention Please!

STORY LEADS

The beginning of a story should get the reader's attention. Circle the introductions that get your attention and make you want to read the rest of the story. Cross out the introductions that do not get your attention.

I bit the sucker. My tooth hurt. I went to the dentist.

It was an awesome lollipop. It changed colors when you licked it. But I never thought I'd have a purple tongue when I went to the dentist with a toothache. I wonder what he thought about that.

Hot dogs are good. I eat them all the time.

How do you like a juicy footlong, fresh off the grill? Ketchup and mustard? Pickles and onion? How about on a toasted bun with the works? Mmmm!

I was sitting by the lake. The duck landed in the water.

I sat by the lake minding my own business, when a loud flapping noise nearly scared me half to death. It was a big old Mallard duck, coming in for a landing.

Write your own attention-getting introductions to replace each of these.

The airplane flew up into the sky.

_____

I like collecting rocks.

_____

Playing soccer is fun.

_____

It was a good movie.

_____

Traits of Good Writing • 4–5 © 2004 Creative Teaching Press

Name _____ Date _____

Let's End Well

STRONG ENDINGS

The way you end a story is very important. A strong story ending will be interesting and should leave the reader feeling satisfied. It should let the reader know that the story has ended without having to say "the end." Look at the story endings below. Draw a star next to the strong endings. Draw a sad face next to the weak story endings.

1 _____ I dropped onto my bed at the end of the day with a smile on my face and fell fast asleep.

2 _____ We had a good day.

3 _____ It was the hardest thing I had ever done, but it was worth every minute of it.

4 _____ Mom was happy that I was home.

5 _____ Jimmy and I looked at each other and both agreed we had never been so scared in our lives, but we loved it.

6 _____ It was a fun time.

7 _____ It was a good field trip.

8 _____ It had been the wildest adventure I'd been on in a long, long, time.

9 _____ The whole family agreed they want to return to the Lost Cave of the Mounds for our next family vacation.

10 _____ It was the most fabulous Friday night we've ever had as a family.

11 _____ Dad and I had fun that day.

12 _____ I never thought I'd be as happy to see my little sister as I was that day.

13 _____ The end.

14 _____ I was dead tired and near tears, but I was glad to be back home with Mom, Dad, and Uncle Jake.

Rewrite two of the weak story endings.

_____

_____

_____

_____

Traits of Good Writing • 4–5 © 2004 Creative Teaching Press

Smooth Transitions

Transitional Words

> **Transitional words and phrases** help connect ideas within and between paragraphs. They do this by showing relationships, such as comparisons, results, or examples.
>
> Example: *similarly* shows comparison or similarity
> *as a result* shows the result of something
> *for example* shows an example

Write the transitional words and phrases under the relationship they show to complete the chart.

also	likewise	to illustrate	consequently	hence
therefore	finally	in brief	in the end	for instance
a case in point	additionally	furthermore	in the same way	equally

addition			
comparison			
example			
result			
summary/conclusion			

Traits of Good Writing • 4–5 © 2004 Creative Teaching Press

Name _____ Date _____

Sequence a Story

STORY SEQUENCE

Read each set of sentences. Order the sentences in each story. Label each sentence with a word from the box.

| Introduction | First | Second | Third | Conclusion |

Michael's Birthday

_____ He and his friends went out for pizza.

_____ It was Michael's tenth birthday party and all his buddies came.

_____ When Michael waved goodbye to his friends, they all wished they could stay longer.

_____ Then they spent a half hour playing laser tag.

_____ Finally, they went to Michael's house for cake and ice cream.

Lucas' Science Project

_____ He named it Benjamin and put it in his shirt pocket.

_____ In science class the turtle peeped its head out of Lucas' pocket, which caused the teacher to scream and send Lucas to the office.

_____ Later on, the teacher decided Lucas could use the new pet turtle as an extra credit research project.

_____ Lucas spotted a turtle in the grass on his way to school.

_____ Lucas got an A in science that year.

Marcus Saves the Day

_____ The team picked up Marcus and carried him around the bases, cheering loudly.

_____ His coach worked with him many days and taught him how to bat.

_____ Marcus got better and better.

_____ Marcus joined the little league baseball team but he had a hard time learning how to bat.

_____ During the championship game, Marcus hit a homerun and won the game.

Think of your own story to write. Write the parts out of order, including a beginning, middle, and conclusion. Invite a classmate to sequence the story.

Traits of Good Writing • 4–5 © 2004 Creative Teaching Press

Name _____ Date _____

In the Doghouse

 EVALUATING A PERSONAL NARRATIVE

A **personal narrative** is a true story that happened to you. When you write a personal narrative you include a beginning that grabs the attention of the reader; tell important events in order; share details about what you felt, thought, heard, and did; and use the pronouns *I*, *me*, and *we*. Your narrative should end by telling how things worked out.

Read the personal narrative and do the following tasks:

• Underline the attention-grabbing beginning.

• Circle the pronouns *I*, *me*, and *we*.

• Write a number next to the sentences that show the order of events. Write a "1" next to the sentence that tells about the first event, a "2" next to the sentence that tells about what happens next, and so on.

• Put a star by words or phrases that give details about what the author felt, thought, or did.

• Draw a box around the part of the story that tells how things worked out.

Have you ever climbed through a doghouse on your hands and knees at 6:30 in the morning, with the dog inside? I did. It all began one morning when my family was eating breakfast. We were just about to clear the table when there was a knock at the door. Who would be here at this early hour? my mother wondered. I wondered the same thing.

When my dad opened the door, there stood Mr. Carlson in his pajamas. I was about to laugh when I heard him say, "I'm locked out of my house. Could one of your girls come over and help me out? I need someone small who can fit inside the doghouse entrance. Then we can get into the garage where there's a key and I can get inside." Unfortunately, I'm the smallest person in the family, so I was nominated for the job.

Dad and I walked over to Mr. Carlson's backyard. I opened the miniature door to the doghouse and wriggled my way through. It wasn't easy. "Here Chester, it's OK," I called nervously, as I looked him in the eye. He was happy to see me. However, I couldn't say the same. I crept along on my hands and knees with Chester close behind me, sniffing all the way. After several uncomfortable seconds, I made it through the small opening into the garage. Mr. Carlson told me where the key was, and I opened the house up for him. I bet he was glad to get inside and change into his clothes.

He thanked me several times. Later that day, Mr. Carlson brought me a package of candy and a small toy for a reward. I thought that was great. Dad said he appreciated my helpful attitude. I was just glad it was over. Dogs and dog cages are not my idea of a fun way to start the day.

Traits of Good Writing • 4–5 © 2004 Creative Teaching Press

Crossword Fun

PARTS OF A STORY

Unscramble the words. Read the clues. Use the unscrambled words to complete the puzzle.

Across
4. How the story ends
5. The most important moment or turning point of the story
7. The main problem in the story
8. The story line

Down
1. The first part of the story
2. The center part of the story
3. The final part of a story
4. The people in the story
6. Where the story takes place

mlciax _____   ddlmie _____   ginbenngi _____

nde _____   ttsngei _____   rahcacsrtes _____

ltop _____   cflction _____   nloucsoni _____

What Is Voice?

VOICE

Use the key to "break the code" and write the letters of the missing word in each sentence.

1 Writing with voice shows you ____ ____ ____ ____ about the message in your writing.
  C4 A3 A4 D3

2 The author uses ___ ___ ___ ___ ___ ___ ___ ___ ___ ___ not just facts.
  D3 B4 D1 A4 D3 D2 D2 C3 B2 B1

3 Writing with voice lets the reader know there's a ___ ___ ___ ___ ___ ___
behind the words.   D1 D3 A4 D2 B2 B1

4 Writers have a ___ ___ ___ ___ ___ ___ way of expressing themselves in their
writing.   A2 B1 C3 B3 A2 D3

5 When writing with voice, authors share their ___ ___ ___ ___ ___ ___ ___ ___
and emotions.   C2 D3 D3 C1 C3 B1 D4 D2

6 Writing with ___ ___ ___ ___ ___ shows there's a real person behind the writing.
  A1 B2 C3 C4 D3

	1	2	3	4
A	V	U	A	R
B	N	O	Q	X
C	L	F	I	C
D	P	S	E	G

Traits of Good Writing • 4–5 © 2004 Creative Teaching Press

Name _____ Date _____

Take Me Out to the Ball Game

RECOGNIZING STRONG AND WEAK VOICE

Read the description of a championship baseball game. Cross out the sentences that have weak voice. Underline the sentences that have strong voice.

We played baseball. It was great how our team came from behind and won the championship game by two runs. The fans were on the edge of their seats. People thought we might lose. We won the game.

Everyone jumped up and cheered when Johnny struck out the last batter. Johnny is a good pitcher. It was a nice baseball game. The fans went wild and so did I. There's nothing better than beating a tough team like the Tigers. Our team had fun. We were happy. Everyone was happy we won. The team was glad to win. The players lifted Johnny into the air and we carried him around the field.

The crowd roared and stomped their feet. It was the best game we ever played. It was a nice game. When I rounded third base, my cap flew off but I didn't stop running. I knew I would make it home. It's nice to win. It was a good baseball game.

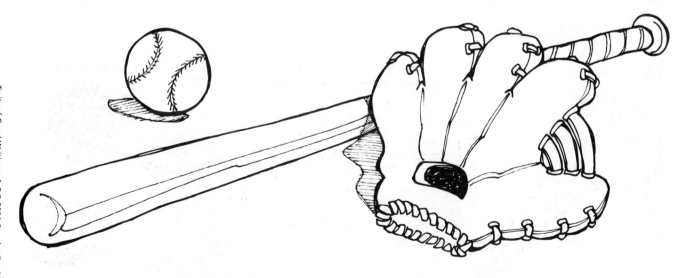

Name _____ Date _____

Learning About Voice

IDENTIFYING VOICE

- Voice adds interest and life to the topic.
- Voice conveys the writer's own style.
- Voice conveys the message that the reader knows about the topic.
- Voice shows the person cares about the topic.
- Voice allows the author's personality to come through.

- Voice shares who you are.
- Voice has natural rhythm.
- Voice includes a good selection of words.
- Voice speaks directly to the reader.
- Voice shows that there's a real person behind the writing.
- Voice draws the reader into the writing.
- Voice conveys feeling and emotion.

Read the statements about a trip to the shopping mall. Circle the sentences that have voice. Cross out the ones that do not have voice.

1 After two hours of shopping, I was so tired I thought I would drop.

2 We shopped a lot.

3 It was fun carrying big shopping bags filled with all our treasures.

4 We all realized that clothes and shoes are very expensive, just like our parents have been saying.

5 Claire's offered fabulous jewelry at prices that I could afford.

6 The food court had so many choices it was hard to decide what to order.

7 We went to the mall.

8 It was fun to sit and listen to the water fountains while we rested and waited for each other.

9 It was a nice time.

10 I had fun picking out a special CD at my favorite music store.

11 We went shopping.

12 I especially liked trying on the fancy, frilly dresses.

13 We learned about spending and saving our hard-earned money.

Traits of Good Writing • 4–5 © 2004 Creative Teaching Press

The Zoo

IDENTIFYING VOICE

Read these sentences. Underline the statements that have voice. Cross out the statements without voice.

We slept at the zoo.

I'd never been to the zoo in the middle of the night before.

We walked in at night.

It seemed unusually quiet and especially dark that night.

I wonder what the reptiles thought of all of us kids sleeping in their building.

We brought sleeping bags.

Jamie and I curled up in our sleeping bags beneath the iguana display.

There were reptiles.

I wondered how many pairs of reptile eyes were watching me sleep.

It was weird to hear the tortoises crawling around in the dark.

Cages of reptiles surrounded us.

We liked sleeping there.

When Jamie said, "We might wake up face-to-face with a boa," I was shaking in my sleeping bag.

It was the most exciting sleepover I've ever been to.

It was a nice sleepover.

 Draw or write about a trip to the zoo. Use voice in your writing.

Coach

STRONG OR WEAK VOICE

Use the words in the word box to complete the sentences in the paragraphs.
Then read the two descriptions of the basketball coach. One paragraph is dull and boring.
It has weak voice. The others have strong voice.

basketball	good	nice	coach	world	conference
Jordan	playing	tough	slacking	improve	sportsmanship
strong	training	mistake	developed	championship	

My _____ coach is Todd Barsness. He is a really _____ coach. He
coaches well. He knows a lot about basketball. He tells us what to do. He's _____.
I like having him for a _____.

I wouldn't trade Coach Barsness for the _____. He's the best in the 5th grade
_____. All the kids on the team say he's an awesome coach, and they mean it.
He's taught our team so many new basketball skills. Coach Barsness said we're "all going
to play like Michael _____ someday." I can already see that I'm _____ a lot
better than last year.

Coach Barsness is _____, too. He really works the team hard. There's no easy
practice or _____ off with him around. Everyone shoots thirty free throws
before practice even begins, and running ten sets of line-grabbers is a part of our daily
_____. Coach says, "That's how we will build a _____ team."

He also teaches us about good _____, respecting our teammates, and obeying the coach's orders. When you make a _____ during a
game he pulls you aside and puts his hand on your shoulder. He says, "Do you know
what happened out there? Then don't worry about it." Then later on he tells us how
to _____.

Coach Barsness has _____ a strong team of basketball players this
year. If we win the conference _____, we owe it all to him.

Traits of Good Writing • 4–5 © 2004 Creative Teaching Press

Dialogue

WRITING A DIALOGUE

When people talk with each other we call their conversation a dialogue. Look at the pictures in each comic strip. Unscramble the words below the comic strips to write the dialogue for each speech bubble.

| is the
ever
A cat
best pet | love snakes
Not for me
I | snakes
snakes
Why | they love
Because
you back. |

| we could
I wish
to school
ride our bikes | ride is
Yeah the bus
always so long —
45 minutes of boredom | no
Oh
tire
Flat | Maybe 45
wasn't so bad
minutes
after all |

First or Third?

PoINT oF VIEW

> **Point of view** shows who is telling the story.
>
> The **first person** point of view means that a character from the story is describing what happened. The story includes the words **I**, **me**, and **we**.
>
> The **third person** point of view means that someone outside the story is describing what happened. This story includes the words **he**, **she**, **they**, or **the name of the character**.

Write **first** or **third** to identify the point of view in each sentence.

1 He ran a mile faster than ever before. _____

2 I was running so fast, I thought I'd trip over my own feet before I reached the finish line. _____

3 Caitlin's mom took her and Emma shopping at the mall. _____

4 We had such a great time shopping together. I hope we can go again next Saturday. _____

5 I thought she might not notice if I slipped into my seat as quickly and quietly as possible. _____

6 Eric thought he could sneak into his seat before the teacher noticed he was late. _____

7 We've always been best friends, but Amanda sure does get jealous when I play with other girls. _____

8 Danielle and Amanda had been friends since preschool, but they still had an argument every now and then. _____

9 I'm so glad Dad got me this new skateboard. I can't wait to try it out at the park with the guys. _____

10 Parker put his new skateboard in his backpack and hopped onto his bike. He headed down to the park to meet his friends. _____

11 Liz and Alyssa each tutored a first-grade student in math and reading skills. _____

12 I can't wait for Lizzy to come and help me with my math again. _____

Traits of Good Writing • 4–5 © 2004 Creative Teaching Press

Name _____ Date _____

Persuade Me

PERSUASIVE WRITING

Persuasive writing is when you write to try to get others to do something or accept your point of view. Persuasive writing requires voice. Without voice, no one will believe your viewpoint.

Circle each statement that has a voice that will persuade someone to agree with the following opinion:

School should end at 1:00 p.m. each day.

1. Children need time off.

2. Families would have more quality time to spend together.

3. Children would have more time to do their homework, and they would probably do a better job on it.

4. School is seven hours long.

5. Children would probably do extra chores at home if they had more free time each day.

6. School isn't fun.

7. Children would learn time-management skills because they would have more time to call their own, and they would learn to be better organized.

8. Children should be at home.

9. Bus drivers would be able to get home earlier in the day to be with their own families.

10. Teachers would appreciate having more time to correct papers and organize the classroom.

11. Children would be less rushed to get to piano lessons, scouts, or soccer practice in the afternoon.

12. Kids get tired.

13. Parents would enjoy having their children around more often.

14. Brothers and sisters wouldn't fight as much because they'd have more time to work out problems and learn how to interact with each other.

Write one more sentence that will persuade a reader to agree with the statement.

_____

Traits of Good Writing • 4–5 © 2004 Creative Teaching Press

Name _____ Date _____

A Treat for the Reader

WORD CHOICE

Look at the pairs of words in these sentences. Circle the word that makes the sentence more precise, descriptive, or interesting.

1 It was a dreary/cloudy day for a field trip to the lake.

2 The dog ran/frolicked on the playground with the kids.

3 We didn't know how the window had been shattered/broken.

4 I saw/spied a tree frog sitting on top of the monkey bars.

5 The kids laughed/chuckled when I told the joke in the hallway.

6 The thermometer read ten degrees below zero; it was a frigid/cold morning.

7 I sat in the reading corner, where it's nice/cozy.

8 Sonja whispered/said, "I think she wants us to raise our hands."

9 Barry's garter snake slithered/moved through the sand and grass.

10 I ran/dashed to the finish line.

11 Mr. Endres ate/devoured his submarine sandwich.

12 She hurled/threw the baseball through the air, and I was out at first base.

13 I tossed/put my jacket in the bottom of my locker and quickly ran into the classroom.

Read the words in the word bank. Write each word beneath the verb it could replace.

| trotted | shouted | crept | spied | announced | tiptoed |
| observed | danced | spotted | studied | declared | exclaimed |

Said	**Went**	**Looked**

Traits of Good Writing • 4–5 © 2004 Creative Teaching Press

Name _____ Date _____

Be Specific
COMMON NOUNS VS. SPECIFIC NOUNS

Using specific nouns makes your writing more interesting. Read each underlined word. Replace each common noun with a specific noun and rewrite the sentence.

1 I put on my <u>shoes</u> to go out in the rain.

_____

2 My father drove me in his <u>car</u> to the <u>restaurant</u>.

_____

3 I saw a <u>dog</u> in the window of the pet store.

_____

4 We ate <u>food</u> for lunch.

_____

5 I had a delicious <u>dessert</u> after dinner.

_____

6 We went into the <u>house</u>.

_____

7 I wore a red <u>hat</u>.

_____

8 My sister can speak two different <u>languages</u>.

_____

Write four more specific nouns here.

_____ _____ _____ _____

A Secret Message

SPECIFIC VERBS

Look at the underlined verb in each sentence. Find a specific verb from the word box to replace each underlined verb. Reread each sentence with the new verb.

earn	skipped	glared	observed	declared	zoomed	won
hike	whispered	constructed	determine	creating	pranced	

1 Mom will <u>see</u> which computer is best for our family. _____

2 Clarissa is <u>making</u> a dollhouse from wood scraps. _____

3 Stacie <u>went</u> to the park to meet her friends. _____

4 Bryce <u>looked</u> at me angrily when I tagged him out. _____

5 We <u>got</u> a prize for the most creative project. _____

6 Rose <u>saw</u> the caterpillar on the tree leaf. _____

7 Annie <u>said</u>, "I knew I could do it. I won!" _____

8 My dad <u>made</u> a new doghouse for Chester. _____

9 Lisa <u>told</u> the secret to a lot of people. _____

10 The boys will <u>go</u> along the trail in the arboretum. _____

11 We can <u>get</u> money by working hard at the farm. _____

12 The doberman <u>ran</u> through the yard. _____

13 The minivan <u>went</u> down our street. _____

The Robot

Specific Verbs

Replace the bold verb in each sentence with a more specific verb from the word box. The first one is done for you.

gathered	created	admired	shouted	discovered	constructed
attached	studied	exclaimed	drew	inserted	declared
ran	glued	hurried	formed		

1 I **saw** the idea in a magazine. _____ *discovered* _____

2 Then, I **read** the instructions for almost an hour. _____

3 I **made** a robot for my science project. _____

4 First, I **got** lots of boxes, cardboard, tubes, tape, and other scrap objects. _____

5 Next, I **made** the arms and legs from cardboard tubes and attached them with duct tape. _____

6 I **made** the head from a chunk of Styrofoam. _____

7 On its head I **made** a face. _____

8 I carefully **put** a flashing light into the head so that the eyes would light up. _____

9 I **put** a walkie-talkie onto the backside of the main body part so that when I spoke it would appear that the robot was talking. _____

10 For details, I **put** buttons, coins, and milk jug lids on the robot to represent nuts and bolts, buttons, electronic dials, and lights. _____

11 I **said**, "This is more fun than I've had in a long time." _____

12 I **went** to tell my mom and dad about the project. _____

13 My mom and dad **came** to see my robot. _____

14 They both **saw** my project. _____

15 Mom **said**, "You did a great job!" _____

16 Dad **said**, "You're definitely going to get an A+ on this." _____

Name _____ Date _____

Adding Adjectives

ADJECTIVES

An **adjective** is a word that describes a noun. Adjectives help create a picture in the reader's mind and make the writing more interesting.

Write one pair of adjectives from the word bank in each sentence to make the sentences more interesting.

leather basketball hot crackling	huge beige gooey sticky	brown leather ice cold	floppy maroon six fuzzy

1. Let's buy this _____ _____ backpack for school.

2. She wore a _____ _____ hat on the field trip.

3. We each drank an _____ _____ beverage after the game.

4. Dad had a _____ _____ fire burning in the fireplace.

5. Justin bought _____ _____ shoes for his first game.

6. The carmel apples were _____ and _____.

7. Sophie collected _____ _____ caterpillars for her science project.

8. They moved into the _____ _____ house on Center Street.

Add two adjectives to each sentence.

9. Maggie wore _____ _____ glasses during the nature walk.

10. Micah and Zach each wore _____ _____ shirts so they would look like twins.

11. Grandma served _____ _____ soup for supper on Sunday night.

12. Kevin played his _____ _____ computer game all afternoon.

13. Drew and Marcus found a _____ _____ ring on the outdoor basketball court.

Traits of Good Writing • 4–5 © 2004 Creative Teaching Press

Antonym Search

ANTONYMS

Antonyms are words that have opposite meanings.

Read each "clue word." Find a matching antonym in the word box. Use the antonyms to complete the crossword puzzle.

imaginary	achieve	local	refreshed
capable	tactful	reject	suddenly
weakened	undependable	repaired	bloom
hastily	vague		

Across
1. wither
3. damaged
4. accept
6. exhausted
8. unqualified
10. carefully
11. obvious
13. gradually

Down
2. real
5. rude
7. foreign
9. fail
12. strengthened
14. trustworthy

Name _____   Date _____

Sunflower Fun

SYNONYMS

> **Synonyms** are words that have the same meaning.

Read the clues. Write the synonym for each in the puzzle.

1. jolly
2. aquaint
3. compose
4. settle
5. beginner
6. preliminary

7. deceptive
8. surplus
9. desolate
10. persuade
11. enthusiastic
12. responsible

1 [ ][ ][ ][ ][ ][ ]

2 [ ][ ][ ][ ][ ][ ][ ]

3 [ ][ ][ ][ ][ ][ ]

4 [ ][ ][ ][ ][ ][ ][ ][ ][ ]

5 [ ][ ][ ][ ][ ][ ][ ]

6 [ ][ ][ ][ ][ ]

7 [ ][ ][ ][ ][ ][ ][ ][ ]

8 [ ][ ][ ][ ][ ][ ]

9 [ ][ ][ ][ ][ ][ ]

10 [ ][ ][ ][ ][ ][ ][ ][ ]

11 [ ][ ][ ][ ][ ]

12 [ ][ ][ ][ ][ ][ ][ ][ ]

festive
eager   reliable
amateur   excess
compromise   dishonest
convince   create
introduce   first
barren

Traits of Good Writing • 4–5 © 2004 Creative Teaching Press

Name _____ Date _____

Get Happy with Homonyms

HOMONYMS

Homonyms are words that sound the same but are spelled differently and have different meanings.

Read each sentence and the homonyms at the right. Write the correct word in each sentence.

1 It took one _____ to clean my bedroom.   hour our

2 She bought new _____ for her vacation.   close clothes

3 _____ like to go along too.   we'd weed

4 _____ you like to ride along?   wood would

5 The _____ class enjoyed the game.   hole whole

6 Smoking is not _____ in the restaurant.   allowed aloud

7 I wanted to _____ over the fence to see the dog.   pier peer

8 The storeowner said it shouldn't cost me another _____ . scent cent sent

9 I didn't know which summer _____ to sign up for.   course coarse

10 I wrapped my sweatshirt around my _____ .   waist waste

11 We all wanted to write about world _____ .   piece peace

12 Mom said that we would go, no matter what the _____ .   weather whether

13 I coasted _____ the tunnel on my mountain bike.   threw through

Write three more pairs of homonyms here.

_____   _____   _____

_____   _____   _____

 Write a paragraph about a happy day in your life. Use some of the homonyms from this page.

Same or Opposite

ANTONYMS AND SYNONYMS

Antonyms = words with opposite meanings
Synonyms = words with the same or similar meanings

Read the pairs of words below. If the words are antonyms, fill in the bubble next to **A**.
If the words are synonyms, fill in the bubble next to **S**.

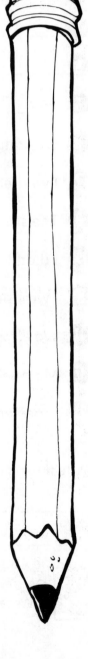

1. harmful   helpful   ○ A   ○ S
2. gather   collect   ○ A   ○ S
3. imitate   copy   ○ A   ○ S
4. calm   peace   ○ A   ○ S
5. infinite   limited   ○ A   ○ S
6. noble   dishonorable   ○ A   ○ S
7. objective   purpose   ○ A   ○ S
8. defy   rebel   ○ A   ○ S
9. damp   wet   ○ A   ○ S
10. appear   disappear   ○ A   ○ S
11. emerge   appear   ○ A   ○ S
12. teach   learn   ○ A   ○ S
13. whole   entire   ○ A   ○ S
14. marvelous   wonderful   ○ A   ○ S
15. repel   attract   ○ A   ○ S
16. revolve   orbit   ○ A   ○ S

Traits of Good Writing • 4–5 © 2004 Creative Teaching Press

Comparisons

Similes

A **simile** compares two things using the word *like* or *as*.

Fill in each blank with a word that completes the simile.

1. She runs as fast as a _____.

2. I am as tall as a _____.

3. Kevin eats so much. He eats like a _____.

4. Leslie barely eats. She eats like a _____.

5. Gordon is as clever as a _____.

6. The view was as pretty as a _____.

7. The girl was as happy as a _____.

8. It happened as quick as a _____.

9. His skin was as smooth as _____.

10. The baby was as cute as a _____.

11. He was as blind as a _____.

12. She was as slow as a _____.

13. The criminal was as sly as a _____.

14. He was as quiet as a _____.

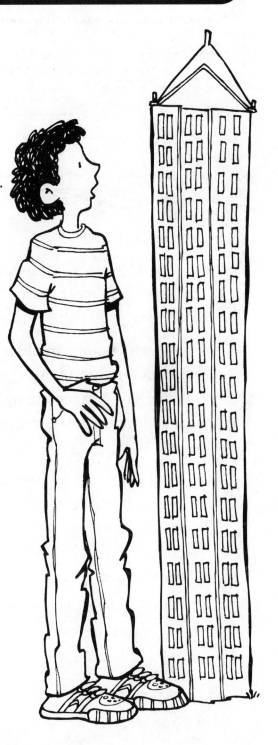

Name _____ Date _____

Write a Postcard

Descriptive Words

Fill in the missing words in these postcards. Which one has more descriptive words and shares more details?

Dear Laura,

I'm sending this _____ from the Milwaukee Museum. It's interesting. It's a _____ place to go. You would _____ it. See you _____.

Anna

like
postcard
soon
nice

Dear Abigail,

The Milwaukee Museum is a _____ place to visit. I'm learning so much about many topics. There's a great display on ancient _____. We even saw a real _____.

We also visited an old town from the early _____ hundreds and got to buy _____ at the General Store. Then we saw a huge display about _____. We climbed inside the skeleton of a _____. We ate _____ for lunch in the cafeteria.

You would have loved the butterfly exhibit. You can walk through a beautiful _____ setting and there are literally hundreds of butterflies in all different shapes, sizes, and colors. A pretty orange _____ butterfly landed on my shoulder.

I hope you and I can visit the museum together sometime this summer.

Your friend,
Anna

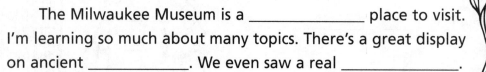

wonderful
monarch
nineteen
cheeseburgers
garden
brontosaurus
Egypt
mummy
dinosaurs
candy

Traits of Good Writing • 4–5 © 2004 Creative Teaching Press

Colorful Captions

Descriptive Words

> A **caption** expresses the content and the mood or emotion of a drawing or photograph. Captions are usually brief (one to three sentences) and contain descriptive words.
>
> Examples:
> weak caption—There is a building in the valley.
> strong caption—The abandoned adobe church lies
> concealed in a valley of fall colors.

Write a caption for each picture.

1

_____

_____

_____

2

_____

_____

_____

3

_____

_____

4

_____

_____

Traits of Good Writing • 4–5 © 2004 Creative Teaching Press

Name _____   Date _____

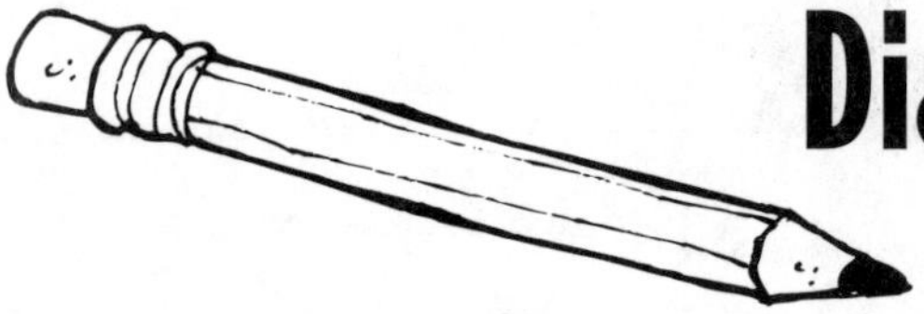

Diamante Poem

DESCRIPTIVE WRITING

A **diamante** poem focuses on two opposite or contrasting subjects. The poem consists of 16 words arranged in seven lines to form a diamond shape.

Choose two opposite nouns. Use descriptive words to fill in the diagram to create a diamante poem.

_____
1st noun

_____,   _____
adjective that describes   adjective that describes
1st noun   1st noun

_____,   _____,   _____
verb that tells what   verb that tells what   verb that tells what
1st noun does   1st noun does   1st noun does

_____, _____, _____, _____
noun associated   noun associated   noun associated   noun associated
with 1st noun   with 1st noun   with 2nd noun   with 2nd noun

_____,   _____,   _____
verb that tells what   verb that tells what   verb that tells what
2nd noun does   2nd noun does   2nd noun does

_____,   _____
adjective that describes   adjective that describes
2nd noun   2nd noun

_____
2nd noun

Traits of Good Writing • 4–5 © 2004 Creative Teaching Press

Persuasive or Not

PERSUASIVE WRITING

> **Persuasive writing** is when you write to try to convince someone to agree with you or to do what you want.

Read each statement. If the sentence uses persuasive writing, write **P**. Write **N** if it does not.

1 _____ Kids should be allowed to ride their bikes to school if they follow all the safety rules.

2 _____ Margaret ate her french fries and drank the entire strawberry shake before she even touched her cheeseburger.

3 _____ You should buy a mountain bike with shock absorbers if you want to ride on rough terrain or trail systems.

4 _____ "Mom, you know I'm responsible and honest. I think I'm old enough to sleep over at Sandra's house for her birthday."

5 _____ "I think I deserve an allowance because I've been doing all my jobs without complaining and I've also proven that I'm wise in spending my money."

6 _____ Jonathan took his little brother to the baseball field for practice.

7 _____ "I've shown that I can take good care of my guinea pig. I would like to ask if I could get one of the puppies that the Kalsows are giving away."

8 _____ All kids should have a Ramrod Remote Control Car. These cars are sturdy, inexpensive, and provide hours of fun for active kids.

9 _____ Nancy asked her parents if she could start using the computer for one half hour each day. She explained how she would play various learning games and practice her typing, not just play games that waste her time.

10 _____ Jeanne picked up the shovel and began digging a hole for the flowers.

11 _____ Maxwell explained how he had worn his bicycle helmet faithfully all summer. He promised to wear one if his parents would buy him a skateboard for his birthday.

Name _____ Date _____

Active vs. Passive

VERB CHOICE

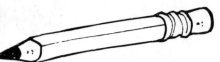

Sentences can be **active** or **passive**. In active sentences, the subject performs the action and the thing receiving the action is the object. In passive sentences, the subject receives the action. Using active voice creates clear and direct sentences. In most writing situations, active voice is preferred. (Note: Passive sentences are not incorrect and actually are effective in some circumstances.)

> Example: During the race, Kathy passed Julie. (active)
> During the race, Julie was passed by Kathy. (passive)

Rewrite each passive sentence to create an active sentence.

1 The boy was stung by a bee.

_____

2 Experiments were conducted by scientists to test the hypothesis.

_____

3 The car is washed by my father.

_____

4 The students are taught by the teacher.

_____

5 Several jokes were told by the comedian.

_____

6 Science and math will be learned by all fourth-graders.

_____

7 The news will be reported by Tom at 5:00 p.m.

_____

8 The phone was answered by the school secretary.

_____

Traits of Good Writing • 4–5 © 2004 Creative Teaching Press

Name _____ Date _____

Adventures in Alliteration

ALLITERATION

Alliteration is used to describe a group of words that share the same beginning sound. Tongue twisters often include alliteration.

Examples: Marsha munched marshmallows at Mary's on Monday.
Pat picks perfect produce for Papa.

Unscramble each set of words to reveal an alliterative sentence.

1 down ran Rex and the rain right Ranger Randi Road in

Rex and Randi _____

2 bat Baxter a Bob big for baseball bought black

Bob Baxter _____

3 Tess Tuesday to tap taught her toes on Thomas

Thomas _____

4 sea sang silly by the sailors seventy songs

Seventy _____

5 first in feasted and french fries the Friday on fish February Fred

Fred _____

Now write your own tongue-twisting sentence.

_____

Traits of Good Writing • 4–5 © 2004 Creative Teaching Press

Name _____ Date _____

Assonance Examples

ASSONANCE

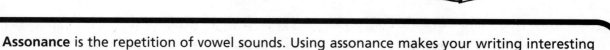

> **Assonance** is the repetition of vowel sounds. Using assonance makes your writing interesting and fun to read.

Read each sentence or phrase. Circle the examples of assonance.

Sue's blue shoes	Keating Street	Wade makes mistakes.
Sleep beneath the trees.	Eat green beans.	Joe saw Sarah.
Bob ate meat.	Vince isn't in.	in the tin bin
high as a kite	Joy pointed at the boys.	Ray paid for Jane.
flying high	I want pizza.	Pet the red hen.
She reads.	Move over, Dad.	Shane makes mistakes.
The boys enjoyed the toys.	five kind guys	Winnie isn't fishing.
Eat at Pete's.	wise guys	rapid traffic

Choose two or more vowel sounds and write several of your own examples of assonance.

_____ _____

_____ _____

_____

Traits of Good Writing • 4–5 © 2004 Creative Teaching Press

Weak or Strong?

WEAK OR STRONG TOPIC SENTENCES

Read the pairs of topic sentences. Circle the topic sentences that use words that grab your attention.

1 I like going to the carnival.   **OR**

Ahhhh, there's nothing like the sights and sounds and smells of the carnival.

2 James took a walk through the park.   **OR**

James didn't mind that the path was leaf-covered, dusty, and not very wide at all, for he was too busy thinking about Bastion.

3 Mom put supper on the table.   **OR**

The crock of chili was piping hot, and the smell of the freshly baked yeast rolls made my mouth water.

4 I found a toad and picked it up.   **OR**

The slippery, slimy creature slipped right out of my hands, so I grabbed it by the legs and then held on tightly.

5 It's fun to work in the garden.   **OR**

There's nothing better than getting dirty and digging and planting in the sweet-smelling, rich, black soil.

6 My friends and I like biking.   **OR**

For the three of us, biking is a time of talking, coasting, popping wheelies, and just riding around hanging out together.

Now read the topic sentences below. Write new topic sentences that will grab the reader's attention. Use words that will make the sentences interesting.

A dog is a nice pet.

_____

A chimpanzee is an interesting animal.

_____

Name _____ Date _____

Know the Characters

CHARACTERS

We can tell a lot about characters by how they think, talk, act, and, sometimes, by how they look. Read each sentence. Write **think**, **talk**, **act**, or **look** to identify the type of character information each sentence contains. Then write down something you can tell about each character from what you read.

1 Sammy looked his mother in the eye. "Mom, I just want you to know that I accidently stepped on the yellow flowers you planted yesterday. I didn't try to, but I slipped when I was kicking the soccer ball."

_____ _____

2 "I think your lunch box is for babies," said Sarah. "When are you going to grow up?"

_____ _____

3 Everyone laughed when Marcie spilled her hot lunch tray, but Jamie quickly got up to help her.

_____ _____

4 "I like your backpack, Janie," commented Trish. She then invited the new girl to ride bikes after school.

_____ _____

5 Mr. Iverson stared at the class with such a frown that his eye brows came together to form one large V. He knew someone had let the snake out of the aquarium.

_____ _____

6 Her hair hung in golden ringlets like sausages from her head. Each ringlet had a frilly pink bow, tied at the top.

_____ _____

7 Polly spent twenty minutes combing her hair and wrapping each pony tail with a colorful band, until she said, "My pony tails are perfect, just like me."

_____ _____

8 Jackson knew he could tackle any boy who joined the team. "I'm ready to scare off anyone who comes near me," he thought to himself.

_____ _____

Traits of Good Writing • 4–5 © 2004 Creative Teaching Press

Name _____ Date _____

Used Very Much

OVERUSED WORDS

The adverb *very* tells a reader that the object or quality is more than usually expected. But because *very* is so overused readers often tend to barely notice the word as they are reading.

Example: The wind blew **very** hard.

The wind blew **exceptionally** hard.

Replace *very* in each sentence with a more descriptive word. Rewrite each sentence with your new word.

1 It was a very hot day.

_____

2 The car moved very slowly.

_____

3 Karen is very intelligent.

_____

4 Derek runs very fast.

_____

5 The shopping bag is very full.

_____

6 That grasshopper jumps very high.

_____

7 The movie was very scary.

_____

8 She parked the car very close to the curb.

_____

9 The bell rang very loudly.

_____

10 I am very tired.

_____

Traits of Good Writing • 4–5 © 2004 Creative Teaching Press

Cinquain Poetry

POETRY

Cinquain poetry is a five-line poem that uses a selection of words to describe something.

Title (one word)
Two words to describe the title
Three words that show action about the title
Four words that show feeling about the title
A synonym for the title

Circle the poems that are cinquains.

Basketball
Round leather
Bouncing Dribbling Shooting
Play it all day
Roundball

Candy, oh candy
I can't get enough
Candy's so sweet
I just love the stuff

Bedroom
Cozy Colorful
Read Sleep Snack
Like to be there
Mine

Trees are so nice
I never think twice
About resting or sleeping
Beneath one

Pick and choose from the words and phrases below to complete this cinquain.
Follow the poetry pattern above.

Cookies

_____ _____

_____ _____ _____

_____ _____ _____ _____

_____

Dessert	It's a great game	Packed with chocolate chunks	Tasty crunchy
Fun	Bake Eat Enjoy	Kick defend score	Bake

Traits of Good Writing • 4–5 © 2004 Creative Teaching Press

Having Fun with Idioms

IDIOMS

An **idiom** is a phrase or an expression that means something different from what the words actually say.

Match each idiom with its meaning.

1 _____ He's on the ball

2 _____ She cracks me up

3 _____ He'll come around

4 _____ I was glued to my seat

5 _____ We laughed our heads off

6 _____ Step on it

7 _____ It's still up in the air

8 _____ Whatever floats your boat

9 _____ She's playing with fire

10 _____ He's in the doghouse

11 _____ I'm going to hit the sack

12 _____ It cost me an arm and a leg

a. It was expensive

b. He's in trouble

c. I'm going to bed

d. He knows what he's doing

e. She makes me laugh

f. He'll agree with us soon

g. Go fast

h. It's still undecided

i. Whatever makes you happy

j. We laughed hard

k. She's doing something dangerous

l. I was so intent on listening that I didn't move

Can you think of an idiom? Write it here.

_____

Name _____ Date _____

 # Bug Off

IDIOMS

Fill in the missing word to complete each idiom. Then match each idiom with its meaning.

| heads | cats | worked | splash | off | hit |
| leg | edge | cut | bit | hands | death |

1 Let's put our _____ together.

a. It's raining hard.

2 Her _____ are tied.

b. Let's think about this.

3 You scared me to _____.

c. Stop bothering me.

4 It's raining _____ and dogs.

d. You scared me.

5 I _____ for days.

e. It was suspenseful.

6 She nearly _____ my head off.

f. Do your best.

7 _____ it out.

g. I worked for a long time.

8 He made a big _____.

h. She talked angrily to me.

9 I was on the _____ of my seat.

i. Stop doing that.

10 Break a _____.

j. She can't do anything about it.

11 Let's _____ the road.

k. He made an impression.

12 Bug _____.

l. Let's go.

Traits of Good Writing • 4–5 © 2004 Creative Teaching Press

In Other Words

DESCRIPTIVE NOUNS

The word box contains descriptive nouns to replace the missing noun "man" in each sentence. Read each sentence and select the most appropriate noun from the box to complete each sentence. Use each word only once.

uncle	postman	doctor	actor	teacher	fireman
salesman	reporter	dad	scientist	brother	repairman

1. We waited for the _____ to come and fix the washing machine.

2. My aunt and _____ visited us last night.

3. The _____ delivered the mail to our neighborhood.

4. My older _____ and I sometimes argue, but we usually get along.

5. The baby cooed as her _____ held her in his arms.

6. The _____ had all of his lines memorized and was ready to shoot his scene.

7. Another patient was waiting to see the _____.

8. The _____ put on his lab coat and goggles before beginning the experiment.

9. I learned how to solve equations from my math _____.

10. The new _____ sold more cars than any other employee.

11. The police officer told his side of the story to the newspaper _____.

12. The _____ put out the blazing fire.

Name _____   Date _____

Baseball

UsING Your Five Senses

Your five senses will help you think of words to describe an event or object. Read this fifth grader's description of a baseball game he attended. Circle the words that pertain to the five senses. Record the words you circle on the chart below.

It was a beautiful breezy summer day at Black Earth Village Park. We were packed into the stadium like sardines. A spattering of colorful blankets lined the grass, saving a spot for people who couldn't find a seat in the bleachers. The smell of fresh popcorn and hot dogs wafted through the air. Everyone stood up and faced the flag as we proudly sang the National Anthem. You could feel the excitement as the teams introduced their players and the village president threw the game ball onto the field. We were playing our longtime rival—the Cross Plains Panthers.

I saw my brother on second base. I waved at him and he waved back. The snap of the bat pierced the air as the game began. The flavors of the ketchup and mustard mingled together on my hot dog. The cola was ice cold and refreshing on a hot summer day. Its sweet flavor cooled my tongue and quenched my thirst. The sun was high in the sky, beating down on us as well as the players. The noon whistle blew loud and clear, as if to say, "It's too hot to be playing baseball." We used whatever we could to cover our heads from the scorching sun.

The game was exciting, tied in the seventh inning. I popped a piece of bubble gum into my mouth and began to chew wildly, hoping to calm my nerves. People cheered and clapped. Parents called out to their sons. We could hear the coaches barking out orders to the players. "OUUTTT" the umpire would shout from behind home plate. Our team was up to bat. Jayden popped a fly ball into the air and dashed toward first base. I breathed a sigh of relief when the outfielder dropped the ball and Jayden was safe. The next batter hit a double, causing one runner to score. That was the final play of the game. We won. Everyone cheered loudly. I squeezed my soda can and crushed it because I was so happy. Everyone agreed it was a great day of fun in the hot sun.

See	Hear	Smell	Taste	Touch or Feel

Traits of Good Writing • 4–5 © 2004 Creative Teaching Press

Name _____ Date _____

Gym Class

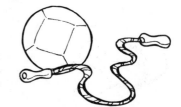

CORRECTING RUN-ON SENTENCES AND FRAGMENTS

The sentences in this girl's essay do not flow smoothly. Look for fragments and run-on sentences. Use these editing marks to edit the page and make the correct changes.

⎓ capitalize   / lowercase   remove   ∧ insert

Gym is my favorite class. In the school day. Mr. Austin is the best gym teacher he plays all the games with us. I won. The jump rope contest. I even beat Jeanne Kurth. When we played kickball. I ran the bases twice I scored two points. I caught. Two fly balls and made two outs. Everyone loves Battle Ball anyone can play it. Volleyball wasn't. My favorite game. Chloe was great. At scoring points. Mr. Austin takes us outdoors for gym in the spring and fall. He taught us about golfing it was hard to learn I couldn't hit the ball very straight at first then he helped me with my swing. Next we'll be learning about bowling we'll learn to keep score. I will look forward to gym class. At the bowling alley. Mr. Austin shows us the ins and outs of all sports. I have more fun in gym. Than in any class. Gym class goes by fast. Because we're having such a good time. When I grow up. I think I'll be a gym teacher. Too.

Traits of Good Writing • 4–5 © 2004 Creative Teaching Press

Name _____   Date _____

Moving Day
VERB TENSE AGREEMENT

Read this story. Look at the boldfaced words. Find a word in the word box to replace each boldfaced word. Cross out the incorrect word in the story and pencil in the correct word.

heard	jumped	exclaimed	won't	raced	sat
have	doesn't	were	didn't	wonder	is
was	hung	having	don't	sat	did
do	replied	unpacked	watched		

Charlie **sit** on the front porch of his new house. "I hope I **has** some friends in this neighborhood. It **didn't** look like any kids live around here," he sighed. Charlie **watch** the movers carry in the couch. "Where **does** you want the sofa?" one man asked his mother. "In the living room is fine," she **reply** with a smile.

Charlie's mom and dad **was** happy to be moving to the new neighborhood, but Charlie **doesn't** share the same feelings. "I already miss my old friends. I **wondered** what Nathan **was** doing right now," he thought to himself. "I bet the old gang is in the tree fort **had** a great time."

Charlie's mom saw his sad face. "Why **didn't** you go up to your new room, Charlie, maybe that will cheer you up." Charlie **does** as he was told. He **sit** on his bed for a while and then **unpack** some of his toys. He thought he **hear** some noise in the backyard and went to look out the window.

Charlie's heart **jumps** in his chest and a huge smile crossed his face. "Wow! I can't believe it!" he **exclaim**. There **were** a big group of kids sitting in his backyard. Balloons and a "Welcome Charlie" sign **hang** from the tree. "Maybe this **wouldn't** be such a bad neighborhood after all," he said as he **race** down the stairs two steps at a time.

Start at the beginning of the story. Look for letters that are marked with an arrow. Print the letters in order in the spaces below to find a hidden message.

___ ___ ___ ___ ___   ___ ___ ___   ___ ___ ___ ___ ___ ___ ___ ___ .

Traits of Good Writing • 4–5 © 2004 Creative Teaching Press

All Together Now

Complete Sentences

You can make complete sentences more interesting by adding details. Look at each group of words. Choose one word or phrase from each group to form six complete sentences. Write your sentences.

Subjects	Predicates	Details
Jennifer	is outside	on Sundays
Nate's bicycle	will sing	with the baby in the stroller
Jacob	is hiding	in the garden planting corn
My cat	opens	a cake for the wedding party
My brother's radio	is closed	under the deck
The zoo	isn't working	at the concert Friday night
Our public library	went swimming	with his friend Ricky
Chef Brussard	is walking	because I broke it by accident
The man	is baking	for the season
Lisa's mother	is working	in the rain

_____

_____

_____

_____

_____

Traits of Good Writing • 4–5 © 2004 Creative Teaching Press

Name _____ Date _____

At the Pond

PARTS OF A SENTENCE

A **complete sentence** needs a subject, a predicate, a beginning capital letter, and an ending punctuation mark.

Circle the subject and underline the complete predicate in each sentence. Then capitalize each beginning letter and add the correct punctuation mark at the end.

1 jason caught six toads

2 tanya picked up a turtle and watched it crawl in the sand

3 hallie found a caterpillar with brown and black fur

4 they will fall in if they walk on those rocks

5 mom caught minnows with a small net

6 i picked up litter and threw it away

7 dad skipped stones on the water

8 hudson found a fishing lure and gave it to me

9 did reba throw away the can after she drank her soda

10 she watched the geese fly in a v formation

11 did bryce scare the ducks away

12 i can't believe you did that

Traits of Good Writing • 4–5 © 2004 Creative Teaching Press

Sentence or Fragment

Complete Sentences

A **complete sentence** has two parts: a subject (noun that the sentence is about) and a predicate (verb that the subject is or did). When a sentence is missing the subject or a predicate we call it a fragment. A **fragment** is a group of words that does not express a complete thought.

Read each example. Fill in the bubble next to **F** if it is a fragment or **S** if it is a complete sentence.

1. ○ F   ○ S   Tons of people everywhere

2. ○ F   ○ S   It was cloudy.

3. ○ F   ○ S   Some people are friendly.

4. ○ F   ○ S   Every other day.

5. ○ F   ○ S   Came over to our house.

6. ○ F   ○ S   Come over here, now.

7. ○ F   ○ S   Every Tuesday, we go to the gym.

8. ○ F   ○ S   Sometimes when it's hot.

9. ○ F   ○ S   Please stay.

10. ○ F   ○ S   Several hundred ants.

11. ○ F   ○ S   The old man and woman.

12. ○ F   ○ S   Kept us warm.

13. ○ F   ○ S   Here is your jacket.

14. ○ F   ○ S   We headed down the mountain.

15. ○ F   ○ S   Pitched a tent.

16. ○ F   ○ S   Talked on the phone for hours.

17. ○ F   ○ S   Teachers are nice.

18. ○ F   ○ S   Many dinosaurs survived.

Traits of Good Writing • 4–5 © 2004 Creative Teaching Press

Make It Complete

COMPLETE SENTENCES

A **complete sentence** has two parts: a subject (noun that the sentence is about) and a predicate (verb that the subject is or did). When a sentence is missing the subject or a predicate we call it a fragment. A **fragment** is a group of words that does not express a complete thought.

Change each fragment into a complete sentence.

1 Early Sunday morning

_____

2 My sister Sarah

_____

3 hit a homerun during the playoff game

_____

4 The antique car

_____

5 ate the entire pizza

_____

6 invited us to her birthday party

_____

7 A ferocious, hungry lion

_____

8 watches television for three hours a day

_____

Traits of Good Writing • 4–5 © 2004 Creative Teaching Press

Name _____ Date _____

Better Beginnings

VARYING SENTENCE BEGINNINGS

To make your writing sound more natural, vary the way you begin each sentence. Which of these groups of sentences sounds better when you read it?

I like horses. I like their manes. I like the way they gallop and jump.
I like horses. Their manes are beautiful. It's exciting to watch them gallop and jump.

Use a word or phrase from the word box to begin each sentence. Then write your own concluding sentence on the last line.

Art class	My favorite	I look forward	It's fun	Students

Art Class

_____ is the best part of the school day.

_____ can create all kinds of projects.

_____ activities are making things from clay and paper-maché.

_____ to art class more than recess.

_____ to make things and display them at home.

_____

I eat	They make	Bananas are	This fabulous fruit	They go

Bananas

_____ the perfect fruit.

_____ great with vanilla ice cream.

_____ bananas all the time.

_____ a perfect topping for crispy rice cereal.

_____ is healthy because it's packed with potassium.

_____

Name _____ Date _____

Compound It

COMPOUND SENTENCES

A **compound sentence** is made up of two simple sentences that are joined together by a comma and a conjunction.

Circle the compound sentences.

1 Alicia rode her bike to the library.

2 Miah went to the store, and then she stopped at the pharmacy.

3 Dana saw the movie.

4 Devin went to the theatre, and then he and his dad ate at McDonald's.

5 She wants to go to the mall for her birthday, or she wants to have friends over.

6 Justin likes bowling, but he thinks soccer is more fun.

7 Casey has a dog, but she says she would rather have a kitten for a pet.

8 Joylin ordered a hamburger, and her mom ordered a vanilla milk shake.

9 Sophie went to her friend's house for lunch.

10 Micah and Zach rode their bikes to the park, but they forgot to stop at the post office to mail the letter.

11 Jose and Darwin had been best friends since preschool, but now they each have new best friends.

Write a compound sentence about yourself.

_____

_____

Traits of Good Writing • 4–5 © 2004 Creative Teaching Press

Name _____ Date _____

Spiders

CONJUNCTIONS, COMBINING SENTENCES

Instead of writing many short sentences, combine your sentences using a conjunction such as *and*, *or*, *but*, *because*, or *although*.

Read each pair of sentences. Determine which conjunction would be best to combine the sentences. Write the conjunction and then make the necessary editing marks to correct the sentence. Read aloud the new sentence. (Note: You might need to change, delete, or add a few other words so the sentence flows smoothly.)

Spiders are creepy. Spiders are interesting to watch.
Spiders are creepy, but they are interesting to watch.

Use these editing marks to revise the sentences: ℘ remove   ∧ insert   / lowercase

1. Spiders have eight legs. _____ Spiders have two body parts.

2. Spiders are helpful. _____ Spiders eat insects.

3. There are many kinds of spiders. _____ Not all kinds live in the United States.

4. Shelly couldn't get to sleep. _____ She saw a spider on the ceiling in her bedroom.

5. Spiders make great pets. _____ Spiders sometimes scare people.

6. One common spider is called daddy long legs. _____ It has very long legs.

7. Justin caught a spider for a pet. _____ His mother would not let him keep it.

8. The spider didn't survive in the jar. _____ It didn't have food or enough air.

9. A spider will tickle you. _____ You have to let it crawl on your arm first.

10. Spiders live outdoors. _____ Spiders live inside your home.

11. People think cobwebs come from spiders. _____ They are simply made from dust gathering in your home.

Name _____ Date _____

Stretch It Out

Descriptive Sentences

Writers use descriptive words to make their sentences more specific and interesting.
>   Before: Mary drank coffee.
>   After: Mary sipped freshly brewed, steamy coffee.

Add descriptive words to "stretch out" each sentence and make it more interesting.

1 Our team won.

_____

2 Carrie ate pizza.

_____

3 The flower is yellow.

_____

4 I like cats.

_____

5 Frank went to the store.

_____

6 She bought a shirt.

_____

7 The lion roared.

_____

8 I read a book.

_____

Traits of Good Writing • 4–5 © 2004 Creative Teaching Press

Birthday Fun

CONJUNCTIONS

Read the sentences. Unscramble the missing conjunction in each sentence and write it in the blank space.

1 I can't wait for the party _____ (secabeu) my friends are coming.

2 I got to choose chocolate _____ (ro) vanilla ice cream.

3 Mom set out the noisemakers _____ (dna) the party hats.

4 I addressed the invitations _____ (erfoeb) mom mailed them.

5 We ate hot dogs _____ (dan) chips.

6 Melissa came, _____ (ghoulath) she lives far away.

7 My puppy wanted cake, _____ (tbu) we didn't give him any.

8 I blew out the candles _____ (cabeseu) Mom wanted to cut the cake.

9 It was a great time, _____ (utb) it seemed to end too quickly.

10 My favorite part of the day was having my friends over _____ (dan) eating Mom's homemade birthday cake.

11 It was a special day _____ (cabeuse) I was with my favorite people.

Write a sentence about a birthday party that you've been to. Use a conjunction in your sentence.

_____

_____

Name _____ Date _____

Bowling

REMOVING UNNECESSARY WORDS

Read the descriptive paragraphs about bowling. The writer sometimes says the same thing or similar things twice. Other times the writer tells about things that don't have to do with the main idea. Cross out the unnecessary words.

Bowling is fun. Bowling is great. There's nothing better than bowling with friends on a Saturday morning. It's great to bowl with friends. We're going to Florida this summer. When you bowl it's important that you choose the right size ball. Using an eight-pound ball is perfect for most fifth graders. Fifth graders should use an eight-pound ball. Twelve pounds is too heavy and six pounds is too light.

You can rent bowling shoes at the bowling alley or you can bring your own. You can use the bowling shoes that are there.

It's important that you bring the ball straight back and let go of it at the right time. When all the pins go down with one roll of the ball, it's called a strike. When you knock over all the pins with two rolls of the ball, it's called a spare. When a ball rolls down the gutter, it's called a gutter ball. Beginning bowlers usually get a lot of gutter balls.

It's important to encourage the kids on your team. My friend Matt is sleeping over this weekend. If someone isn't doing so well, you should encourage him or her. It's fun to take a break between games and eat hot French fries and drink soda or ice cold juice. The French fries are hot. The juice is cold.

We spend a lot of time laughing when we bowl together. It's a good time to gather with family or friends. We laugh a lot when we bowl.

Bowling is good exercise and it helps you stay fit. It's better than watching cartoons on Saturday morning. I'd rather bowl than watch cartoons on Saturdays.

Traits of Good Writing • 4–5 © 2004 Creative Teaching Press

At the Restaurant

EXPANDING SENTENCES WITH ADJECTIVES

Add an adjective(s) from the word box to make each sentence more interesting and meaningful.

fifteen long	cheerful	lemon iced	fanciest
long wooden	Chinese chicken	tall plastic	hot ham
ice cold	grilled cheese	chocolate	
fancy ice cream	generous	best	

1 We waited _____ _____ minutes before we were seated.

2 We sat at a _____ _____ table.

3 The _____ waitress took our order.

4 Ben ordered a _____ _____ sandwich.

5 Mrs. Murray drank _____ _____ tea.

6 The waitress poured water into _____ _____ glasses.

7 Bobby drank _____ milk.

8 Most of the children ordered _____ _____ sodas.

9 Jill's mom had a _____ _____ salad.

10 I ordered _____ _____ on rye bread.

11 Some children ordered _____ _____ _____ desserts.

12 We remembered to use our _____ manners.

13 Everyone wore their _____ clothes.

14 We left a _____ tip for the kind waitress.

Name _____ Date _____

Ice Cream

FOUR KINDS OF SENTENCES

A **declarative** sentence tells about something and ends with a period.
An **interrogative** sentence asks something and ends with a question mark.
An **imperative** sentence gives an order and ends with a period.
An **exclamatory** sentence expresses strong feeling and ends with an exclamation point.

Read each sentence. Write **declarative**, **interrogative**, **imperative**, or **exclamatory** to identify the type of sentence.

1. My Uncle Mike works at Sweet's Ice Cream Factory. _____

2. He often brings us big bags full of ice-cream treats. _____

3. Mint chocolate chip ice cream is out of this world! _____

4. Put it in the freezer. _____

5. There are many flavors of ice cream to choose from. _____

6. I love ice cream treats! _____

7. What is your favorite flavor? _____

8. Many people like chocolate chip cookie dough ice cream. _____

9. Don't let it melt. _____

10. Another popular flavor is called cookies and cream. _____

11. It has chunks of crushed-up sandwich cookies mixed in
    with the ice cream. _____

12. Did you know that ice cream is made from milk and has
    a lot of calcium? _____

Traits of Good Writing • 4–5 © 2004 Creative Teaching Press

Name _____ Date _____

Cousins

PUNCTUATING SENTENCES

Read the letters written by two cousins. Add end punctuation for each sentence so that the sentences flow smoothly.

Dear Gibson,

How are you doing I haven't heard from you in a long time Write to me How is your family We're doing fine in Wisconsin Spring is here and it's a lot warmer now Everyone is wearing shorts to school because its sixty degrees I can't wait for summer You have to see my new skateboard It's the coolest I'm getting pretty good at riding it Buy one You'll love riding it after school each day

Next week we have spring break I can't wait We're going to a movie on Monday and then out for pizza On Friday my dad is off from work so we'll do something together like fishing or hiking How about you When do you have spring break

Last week we started soccer practice Our first game will be next weekend Soccer is the coolest sport

I'm looking forward to seeing you at the family reunion this summer I hope we get to go boating and fishing again this year I knew I'd catch a bigger fish than you Have fun Write back

Thomas

Dear Thomas,

I bet I can outfish you this year I have a new pole and some great new tackle Not much is going on around here We had spring break last week It was fun It was great to sleep late every day We visited Grandma She's doing well Write to her She misses seeing you

I rode on a skateboard once No thanks I had more bandages on my knees and legs than you could count I'll stick to biking My dad bought a new seat and shock absorbers for my bike I love riding over the hills in the field and jumping over the ramps we built last summer

Say hi to your family See you at the reunion The fishing contest begins at 6:00 a.m. that Saturday morning Be ready

Gibson

Traits of Good Writing • 4–5 © 2004 Creative Teaching Press

Let's Go to the Movies

IMPERATIVE SENTENCES

An **imperative sentence** is a command. In an imperative sentence, *you* is always the subject and it is usually not stated in the sentence.

Rearrange each set of words to create an imperative sentence. Remember to start each sentence with a verb.

1 a seat find we can where see

_____

2 to the supper movie go before

_____

3 screen your keep eyes on the

_____

4 before your eat the movie popcorn starts

_____

5 close the sit the to theater center of

_____

6 spill don't soda your

_____

7 here wait

_____

8 the tickets buy

_____

9 be afraid don't

_____

10 your comfortable get in chair

_____

11 the previews enjoy the show before

_____

Traits of Good Writing • 4–5 © 2004 Creative Teaching Press

Name _____ Date _____

Happy Holidays

CAPITALIZATION OF HOLIDAYS AND MONTHS

Answer the questions by writing the month or holiday in each blank.

1 The month in which we celebrate
Martin Luther King Jr.'s birthday

_____

2 The holiday in November when families gather
to give thanks

_____

3 The holiday when many people dress in costumes
and go from door to door to receive candy

_____

4 The holiday when we honor George Washington
and Abraham Lincoln

_____

5 The holiday when people send cards and flowers
or candy to others

_____

6 Another name for the fourth of July

_____

7 Thanksgiving falls during this month

_____

8 The month when people celebrate Christmas

_____

9 The first holiday of each year

_____

10 The holiday when people try to fool each other

_____

11 The month in which we celebrate Independence Day

_____

12 The month in which we celebrate Valentine's day

_____

13 The eighth month of the year

_____

Write your favorite holidays or months of the year here.

_____   _____

_____   _____

Name _____ Date _____

My Favorites

Write each name from the word bank beneath the matching heading. Be sure to capitalize each proper noun. Add one of your own favorites to each category.

froot loops	pizza hut	runaway ralph	green bay packers	holes
frosted flakes	seattle seahawks	parent trap	new york yankees	chicago
star wars	san diego zoo	burger king	mcdonald's	snickers
harry potter	los angeles lakers			

Favorite Cereals and Snack Foods

Favorite Books and Movies

Favorite Cities and Places to Visit

Favorite Restaurants

Favorite Sports Teams

Name _____ Date _____

School Rules

SPELLING

A fourth-grade boy wrote this list of school rules but forgot to proofread it. Circle all the misspelled words.

1 Students may chew buble gum during math class.

2 Students are to jump up and down and showt out lowd when they get an A on a quizz or test.

3 All children will eat snaxs, including cheese and krackers, during silent reading.

4 The teecher must raize her hand when she wants to ask a studunt a question.

5 Students may bring their pilows to school in case they get tried during reading.

6 After gym class every child gets a free can of pop from the teachers' lounnge.

7 The students make a new seeting arraingement every Monday.

8 Students get to relacks in the teachers' lounge when they finnish there work.

9 Students may listen to their favorite CDs in muzic class.

10 A therty minute reces will be held every our on the hour.

11 When it's your berthday, the school will order piza for the whole class at lunch time.

12 Children can talk on cellular phones with frends in other classrooms.

Traits of Good Writing • 4–5 © 2004 Creative Teaching Press

What's That Buzz?

USING QUOTATION MARKS

Read each sentence. Add quotation marks and commas as needed.

1 This is a great day for a walk through the field declared Greg.

2 It's nice of your parents to take us on a hike added Jose.

3 Yeah, my parents are pretty cool replied Greg.

4 Marcie said, Look out for that beehive. It's huge.

5 I hate bees! replied Jose.

6 Me too exclaimed Greg. I remember when my little brother got stung. He cried for a long time.

7 I bet it hurts a lot answered Marcie.

8 My mom says they won't bother you, if you don't bother them replied Jose.

9 Greg's mom smiled and whispered I remember when two bees stung your dad.

10 Don't remind me exclaimed Dad.

11 I think I'll stand over here declared Greg.

12 Me too! exclaimed Jose.

Traits of Good Writing • 4–5 © 2004 Creative Teaching Press

Name _____ Date _____

School Days

PUNCTUATION AND CAPITALIZATION

Add the correct capitalization and ending punctuation to each sentence. Use editing marks to make your revisions.

1 Are you buying a Hot or cold lunch today

2 sarah didn't finish her homework

3 Wow That was the hardest Test I've ever taken

4 sheila's locker wouldn't open

5 Can we call mr. marx to help open the locker

6 Who's your Teacher this year

7 Fire Drill Everybody line up

8 Would you like to play soccer at recess

9 art class is my favorite time of day how about you

10 what time is recess

11 The Bus ride was too long

12 Do you want milk or juice

13 stephanie and miles think Gym class is the best

14 What is the new Music teacher's name

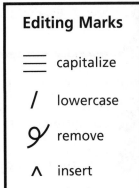

Editing Marks	
=	capitalize
/	lowercase
ℐ	remove
∧	insert

Write three sentences or questions about school. Be sure to use correct punctuation and capitalization.

_____

_____

_____

Traits of Good Writing • 4–5 © 2004 Creative Teaching Press

Name _____ Date _____

Pet Guinea Pig

USING SEMICOLONS

> A **semicolon** can be used in place of a comma and a conjunction to separate the independent clauses in a compound sentence.
>
> Example: A pet goldfish did not interest her; she wanted a pet she could hold and cuddle.

Add a semicolon to each sentence.

1 Guinea pigs are excellent pets they require very little time and attention.

2 Caring for a guinea pig is very simple you just have to feed it, hold it, and love it.

3 Guinea pigs enjoy attention they love being held and caressed.

4 Guinea pigs like to hide under some kind of shelter a shoe box, a plastic container, or a store-bought wooden bridge are all good choices.

5 Sometimes your pet will give a sign that it wants your attention he or she will squeak when you enter the room.

6 A guinea pig's diet is very simple all it requires are carrots, grass or hay, and guinea pig pellets.

7 Their habitat is easy to manage just change the cedar shavings in their cage once a week.

8 Guinea pigs are quiet animals most of the time they sit and relax in their cage for much of the day.

9 Guinea pigs enjoy various activities they like walking outdoors, running around the house, and chewing on chew sticks.

10 Guinea pigs are contented animals they are happy to be alone, with people, or with other friendly guinea pigs.

11 A carrot is a favorite treat for most guinea pigs just place one in the cage, and they'll eat it right away.

Name _____ Date _____

Careful with Commas

Using Commas

Add commas as needed to each sentence.

1 Andy Drew and Joe came over after school.

2 The boys hung up their coats hats and backpacks.

3 Joe did his chores and Drew and Andy helped.

4 We played soccer baseball and checkers.

5 We ate crackers cheese and popcorn for a snack.

6 We passed dribbled and dunked the basketball.

7 "Boys time to come in for supper" called Mrs. Murray.

8 "Okay we're coming" replied Joe.

9 Joe's mom served pizza carrots and garlic bread for supper.

10 Drew did his math homework and Andy and Joe finished the science project.

11 "Yes we'd like to come over tomorrow too" declared Andy and Drew.

12 Joe showed his rock collection to Andy and Drew looked at Joe's robot collection.

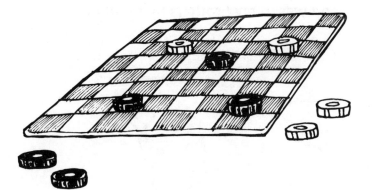

Name _____ Date _____

At the Beach

USING APOSTROPHES

Add apostrophes as needed in each sentence.

1 Jennifers swimsuit has red and white stripes.

2 Were all going for a swim.

3 Moms sun hat has pink flowers all over it.

4 Jacobs sand castle had a flag on top.

5 Shes going to float on an air mattress.

6 Dads blowing up the inner tube.

7 I sat on my dads towel.

8 Hes practicing the backstroke.

9 Were all putting on sunscreen.

10 We didnt have trouble finding Olbrich Beach.

11 Were going to eat lunch in the shade.

12 Theyre carrying the blanket and basket over there.

13 There were sand pails and shovels on all the childrens towels.

14 The sand was in my brothers hair and his swimsuit.

15 Josiah wore Moms sunglasses.

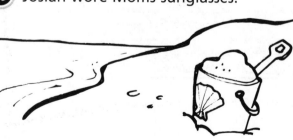

Traits of Good Writing • 4–5 © 2004 Creative Teaching Press

Pen Pal

Misspelled Words

Read the letter Matthew wrote to his pen pal. Cross out each misspelled word and write the correct spelling above it.

Dear Chang,

How are you doin? I haven't herd from you in a long time. I'm doin

well. In scool we are learning about your cuntry, China. I bet it's fun to

live their. My family and I ate at a Chinese resterunt last weekend. I thout

about you. I had chiken and rice. It was grate. I playyed soccer on Satirday.

We lost, but I had fun inyway. I can't rember if I told you, but I got a new

skatboard for my berthday in Novumber. Do you hav skatboards in China?

I also have inline skates, but I like skateboarding beter. We have a big

driveway, so I can skate on the drivway anytime. What do you like doing

for funn? Not much else is new here except that my dad got a new job.

He works in a bigger ofice and it's farthur away, so he gets home a lot later

than usuall. By the way, what dues your dad do for work?

I hop you rite back soon.

Sincerely,

Matthew

Traits of Good Writing • 4–5 © 2004 Creative Teaching Press

Shelley's Spelling List

MISSPELLED WORDS

Correctly write each misspelled word. Then fill in the blanks below with the correct letters to find a special message.

1 educaton
⎯ ⎯ ⎯ ⎯ ⎯ ⎯ ⎯ ⎯ ⎯
　　12

2 continant
⎯ ⎯ ⎯ ⎯ ⎯ ⎯ ⎯ ⎯ ⎯
　　　　6

3 ennergy
⎯ ⎯ ⎯ ⎯ ⎯ ⎯

4 gravitty
⎯ ⎯ ⎯ ⎯ ⎯ ⎯ ⎯
8

5 blizard
⎯ ⎯ ⎯ ⎯ ⎯ ⎯ ⎯
　4

6 atic
⎯ ⎯ ⎯ ⎯ ⎯

7 beehind
⎯ ⎯ ⎯ ⎯ ⎯ ⎯
　　　7

8 paragraf
⎯ ⎯ ⎯ ⎯ ⎯ ⎯ ⎯ ⎯ ⎯
　　　　　　2

9 mayer
⎯ ⎯ ⎯ ⎯ ⎯

10 importint
⎯ ⎯ ⎯ ⎯ ⎯ ⎯ ⎯ ⎯ ⎯
　　　　　　13

11 peice
⎯ ⎯ ⎯ ⎯ ⎯
　　3

12 slipery
⎯ ⎯ ⎯ ⎯ ⎯ ⎯ ⎯ ⎯
1

13 recieve
⎯ ⎯ ⎯ ⎯ ⎯ ⎯ ⎯
　　　9

14 alow
⎯ ⎯ ⎯ ⎯ ⎯
　　5

15 reson
⎯ ⎯ ⎯ ⎯ ⎯ ⎯
　　　10

16 fritened
⎯ ⎯ ⎯ ⎯ ⎯ ⎯ ⎯ ⎯ ⎯
11

⎯ ⎯ ⎯ ⎯ ⎯ ⎯ ⎯ ⎯　⎯ ⎯　⎯ ⎯ ⎯ !
1　2　3　4　5　6　7　8　　9　10　　11　12　13

Traits of Good Writing • 4–5 © 2004 Creative Teaching Press

Lunchtime

WRITING COMPLETE SENTENCES

A complete sentence has a subject and a predicate. A **subject** is the part of the sentence that names a person, place, or thing. The **predicate** is the part of the sentence that tells what the subject is or does.

Circle the complete subject and underline the complete predicate in each sentence.

1. The chocolate milk is very cold.

2. This Granny Smith apple is crunchy and sour.

3. My cherry juice box spilled all over the table.

4. I like tuna sandwiches with lettuce on top.

5. I ate my chocolate cupcake before my sandwich.

6. Mom packed carrots and dip in my lunch.

7. Strawberry-banana yogurt is one of my favorites.

8. Crunchy corn chips are the best part of lunchtime.

9. Peanut butter sandwiches are always good with jelly or bananas.

10. The granola bar was apple flavored.

11. I stacked sliced cheese on my saltine crackers.

12. The turkey sandwich was great on rye bread.

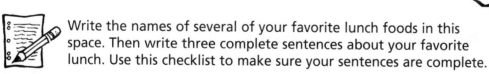
Write the names of several of your favorite lunch foods in this space. Then write three complete sentences about your favorite lunch. Use this checklist to make sure your sentences are complete.

My Favorites

❑ My sentence has a subject. I circled it.
❑ My sentence has a predicate. I underlined it.
❑ I capitalized the first word in the sentence.
❑ I used ending punctuation.
❑ My handwriting was neat.
❑ I used adjectives or adverbs to make the sentence interesting.

Spaghetti Is Best

SUBJECTS, SIMPLE SUBJECTS, AND PREDICATES

> The **simple subject** is a noun or pronoun. It's the most important word in the complete subject.

Underline each subject. Circle the word that is the simple subject. Draw a rectangle around each predicate. The first one is done for you.

1 Spicy meat and mushroom (spaghetti) is my favorite meal.

2 Parmesan cheese is a tasty topping to sprinkle on the spaghetti.

3 My mom makes the best spaghetti in the world.

4 My family usually eats spaghetti on Wednesday nights.

5 My older brother would eat spaghetti every day if my parents would let him.

6 My little sister always gets sauce on her face and in her hair.

7 The meatballs are my favorite part.

8 My dad usually ends up getting sauce on his shirt.

9 Hot buttery garlic bread is another food that goes great with spaghetti.

10 My mom says I must be part Italian.

11 The slippery long noodles are fun to twirl on your fork.

Traits of Good Writing • 4–5 © 2004 Creative Teaching Press

Name _____ Date _____

Pizza Party

SIMPLE PREDICATES

The **simple predicate** is the main word in the predicate. The simple predicate is always a verb. The other words in the predicate tell about this verb.

Read each sentence. Underline the predicate and then circle the simple predicate.

1 Matthew loves pepperoni pizza.

2 My family eats at the Pizza Plaza almost every week.

3 Jordan says olives are his favorite topping.

4 Jacqueline discovered a new pizza place at the mall.

5 We travel to the Pizza Pit-Stop whenever we're in town.

6 My grandma orders pizza from Charlie's Diner.

7 Mr. Manning stopped for carryout pizza.

8 They built a new pizza restaurant on Maple Street.

9 The girls walked to the Pizza Palace.

10 Isaac and David bought a frozen pizza from Gander's Grocery.

11 My brother works at the Pizza Shop.

12 Barry and I order pizza for lunch sometimes.

13 My brother always gives my sister the biggest slice.

Name _____   Date _____

At the Carnival

DIRECT OBJECTS

A **direct object** is the noun or pronoun that receives the action of the verb. Direct objects always follow action verbs.

The verb is underlined in each sentence. Circle the direct object. Draw an arrow from the verb to the direct object.

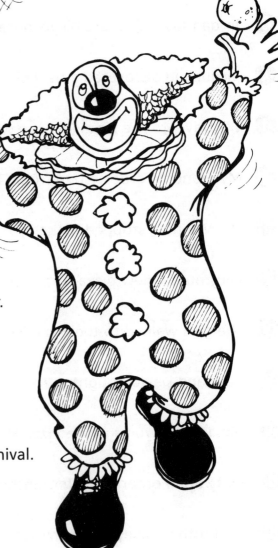

1. My whole family <u>enjoyed</u> the carnival.

2. The clown <u>juggled</u> five oranges at one time.

3. Jenny <u>ate</u> all her cotton candy.

4. My parents <u>bought</u> a large pizza.

5. I <u>drank</u> a tall glass of ice cold soda.

6. Jason and I <u>played</u> games on the midway.

7. Dad <u>won</u> a prize at the ring toss game.

8. Mom and I <u>rode</u> three different rides together.

9. We <u>watched</u> a fireworks display at night.

10. Dad <u>ordered</u> footlong hot dogs for everyone.

11. My family <u>spent</u> twenty-five dollars at the carnival.

Traits of Good Writing • 4–5 © 2004 Creative Teaching Press

Name _____ Date _____

Bedroom Bonanza

PREPOSITIONAL PHRASES

A **prepositional phrase** begins with a preposition such as *in, of, on, under, to, through, from, around,* or *about*.

Read each sentence. Underline the prepositional phrase in each sentence.

1 His computer game is under the bed.

2 His favorite sweatshirt is lying on the floor.

3 Jeremiah's mom is standing in the doorway.

4 The toys on the shelf are new.

5 Jeremiah found his book from the library.

6 The game pieces on the floor are broken.

7 The skateboard should go in the garage.

8 The dirty clothes should be in the hamper.

9 His boom box is on the bed.

10 The crayons on the table are his.

11 The hangers are on the closet floor.

12 The hamster is running around the bedroom.

13 The pillow is under the toy shelf.

Computer Match-Up

PARTS OF A SENTENCE, PARTS OF SPEECH

Print the term from the word bank that matches the definition on the computer screen.

1 A word that shows action

_____

2 A punctuation mark at the end of a question

_____

3 A word that describes a verb

_____

4 A person, place, thing, or idea

_____

5 A specific word that takes the place of a noun

_____

6 A word that describes a noun

_____

7 The part of a sentence that tells who or what the sentence is about

_____

8 The part of a sentence that tells what the subject is or does

_____

9 The noun or pronoun that receives the action of the verb

_____

10 A sentence that gives an order

_____

11 A sentence that shows strong feelings

_____

12 A word that joins two simple sentences together to make a compound sentence

_____

verb	conjunction	adverb	noun
adjective	subject	direct object	command
question mark	predicate	proper noun	exclamation

Traits of Good Writing • 4–5 © 2004 Creative Teaching Press

Name _____ Date _____

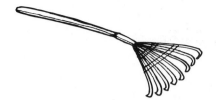

Yard Work

RUN-ON SENTENCES

Read each run-on sentence. Write two or three shorter sentences so that the sentences sound more natural and less confusing. You may need to add or delete words.

1 Mom raked up the grass and trimmed the bushes and picked up twigs.

_____

2 Mr. Lord let us use his weed trimmer and two of his shovels and he showed us how to plant a tree.

_____

_____

3 James took off his jacket and helped his dad and carried the trash bag and the tools.

_____

4 I dug up the weeds and planted a bush and helped Mom plant tulips.

_____

5 Dad wanted to mow the lawn and put down fertilizer and we picked up any litter we could find.

_____

_____

6 My sister helped rake the leaves and she brought out lemonade and she brought out cookies and asked Dad if we were almost finished with the work.

_____

_____

Traits of Good Writing • 4–5 © 2004 Creative Teaching Press

In the City

Run-on Sentences

A **run-on sentence** is when two or more sentences run together.

Add punctuation and capital letters to correct these run-on sentences.

1 The stores are open early it's a busy day in the city.

2 Many cars are stopped the people honk their horns.

3 Many people cross the street it's a busy corner.

4 It's noisy in the city the dogs bark loudly.

5 The shoppers carry packages they are having fun.

6 Two men walk into the restaurant they're going to eat lunch.

7 The woman talks on her cell phone she's on her way home.

8 Mr. James sweeps off the steps he puts a sign in the window.

9 The boys walk on the sidewalk each one has a package.

10 Mrs. Murray has her dog on a leash I hope it doesn't get away it's a big dog.

11 The storeowner opened the shop he let the people in early.

12 Shopping in the city is fun it's a very busy place.

13 People on bikes wait to cross the road they're all wearing helmets.

14 The officer helps direct traffic everyone goes around the construction workers.

Traits of Good Writing • 4–5 © 2004 Creative Teaching Press

Name _____ Date _____

At the Mall

DEMONSTRATIVE ADJECTIVES

This, *that*, *these*, and *those* can be used as demonstrative adjectives. Circle the demonstrative adjective in each sentence.

1. Do you want to try on those pants?

2. "I want this baseball hat, Dad."

3. How about if we buy these socks?

4. We should buy that CD.

5. "The heel on those shoes is too high," declared Mom.

6. This store might have cool tennis shoes for me.

7. This watch is too expensive.

8. We should get these striped socks.

9. Great! This store has a candy aisle.

10. "Mom likes this sweater," Marissa told Dad.

11. "These ice-cream cones are great, aren't they kids?"

12. This mall is a fun place to shop.

Cross out each demonstrative adjective below as you circle it in the sentences above. You will find a special message. Write the message on the lines.

HTHATATHESEVTHISETHOSEFTHOSEUTHISNSTHISHTHESEOTHISPTHESEPTHISINTHISG

___ ___ ___ ___ ___ ___ ___ ___ ___ ___ ___ ___ ___ ___!

Name _____ Date _____

Just a Note

WORD USAGE

Rewrite these notes using the correct word to replace each boldfaced word.

Dear Mom,

Mimi called to see if I could **came** over. I **gone** to her house to try her new computer game. I **has** my homework with me. I hope you **didn't** mind that I'm **went**.

Love, Sophie

Dear Mom,

_____

_____

_____

_____

_____

Love, Sophie

Joe,

Do you **has** the book I **given** you? I **come** over to borrow it, but you **was** gone. I **were** hoping you'd be home. Can I **came** over when you **got** home?

Toby

P.S. You **has** to see my new skateboard!

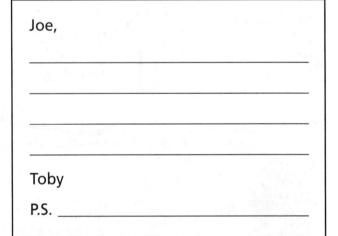

Joe,

_____

_____

_____

_____

Toby

P.S. _____

Mr. Boston,

We **has** your mail. The postman **given** it to us when you **was** gone. We can **came** over when you **got** home.

The Murrays

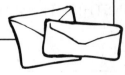

Mr. Boston,

_____

_____

_____

The Murrays

Traits of Good Writing • 4–5 © 2004 Creative Teaching Press

Name _____   Date _____

Birthday Party

SINGULAR AND PLURAL NOUNS

Read about Sophie's birthday party. Look at the underlined nouns.
Write each noun underneath the correct heading.

1 Sophie was having a special birthday <u>party</u>.

2 She invited seven <u>friends</u> to come to her house.

3 All the <u>kids</u> arrived at 3:00 p.m.

4 Her mom baked a triple-decker, chocolate layer <u>cake</u>.

5 The children all brought <u>presents</u> for the birthday girl.

6 Everyone enjoyed two <u>scoops</u> of ice-cream with their cake.

7 Joseph put on a party <u>hat</u>.

8 Everyone sang the birthday <u>song</u> to Sophie.

9 Ali gave Sophie two computer <u>games</u>.

10 The party <u>favors</u> were a big hit.

11 Everybody won a <u>prize</u>.

12 The children played in the tree <u>house</u> after that.

13 Sophie wrote seven thank-you <u>notes</u>.

Singular Nouns

_____   _____

_____   _____

_____   _____

_____   _____

Plural Nouns

_____   _____

_____   _____

_____   _____

_____   _____

Person, Place, Thing, or Idea

NOUNS

A **noun** is a person, place, thing, or idea. A **proper noun** names a specific item and begins with a capital letter.

Circle the nouns in each sentence and then write in the space above the word if the noun is a person, place, thing, or idea. Underline all proper nouns.

1 Shelly walked in the door and smiled at me.

2 During math class, Justin sneezed so loud that the teacher jumped out of her chair.

3 Benjamin is always chewing gum in math class.

4 Mr. Kenny, the gym teacher, couldn't find his whistle.

5 Ms. Darst displayed my clay pot as an example for the class.

6 I enjoy singing movie theme songs in music class.

7 My sister Sophia enjoyed reading the book *Holes*.

8 Trevor searched his backpack, but he couldn't find his homework.

9 Mr. Williams asked me to clean my locker before we said the Pledge of Allegiance.

10 On the last day of school, we always have Field Days events.

11 My favorite games are tug-of-war and the water-balloon toss.

Name _____ Date _____

Dear Uncle Dave

PAST TENSE VERBS

Read this letter that Justin wrote to his uncle. Then help him finish the letter by printing the past tense verb on each line.

Dear Uncle Dave,

    I'm sorry you _____ (miss) my soccer game. We beat the Tigers

six to three. It _____ (is) the coolest game ever. I _____ (score) two

goals. My friend Alan _____ (score) two goals also. I _____ (run)

as fast as I could and _____ (kick) the ball more than ever before.

I _____ (play) goalie, too. I _____ (is) a good defender. My coach

put me in all four quarters of the game. Mom and Dad _____ (laugh)

when I fell down. I _____ (laugh), too. I _____ (rest) during

half time. Boy, was I tired. Allie _____ (watch) the game from her

stroller. When the whistle _____ (blow) at the end, I _____ (jump)

up and down. Mom _____ (clap). Dad _____ (throw) his hat

into the air. I _____ (cheer) as loudly as I could. The whole team

_____ (play) a great game. I hope you can come to my next game.

Justin

 Write a letter to someone you know. Tell the person about a game you played or watched. Use several past tense verbs as you write.

Name _____ Date _____

Skates and Skateboards

ARTICLES

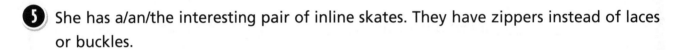

A, *an*, and *the* are special adjectives called articles.

Circle the correct article in each sentence.

1 A skateboard is a/an/the great birthday gift.

2 A/An/The wheels on my inline skates are wearing down.

3 I love riding a skateboard on a/an/the hot summer day.

4 There's nothing like coasting down a/an/the hill.

5 She has a/an/the interesting pair of inline skates. They have zippers instead of laces or buckles.

6 His skateboard is a/an/the best money can buy.

7 It's easier to skate on a/an/the pair of inline skates than regular roller skates.

8 It's fun to skate indoors or outdoors with a/an/the friend.

9 Riding on a skateboard is like riding on a/an/the wind.

10 It's cool to ride up a ramp and hop over a/an/the edge.

11 Landing on your feet is a/an/the tricky part.

12 Riding a skateboard is a/an/the inexpensive way to have fun.

13 An/The roller rink is a great place to skate.

14 She is a/an/the excellent inline skater.

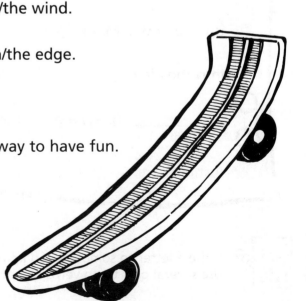

Traits of Good Writing • 4–5 © 2004 Creative Teaching Press

Name _____ Date _____

Tic-Tac-Toe

ADJECTIVES AND ADVERBS

Look at the boldfaced words on the tic-tac-toe grids. Color in the space if the boldfaced word is an adjective. Try to get three in a row.

The **long** pencil broke.	The raccoon grew a **thick** coat.	She had **curly** hair.
He wore a **black** cap.	They jogged **together**.	We **quickly** folded the papers.
He listened **carefully**.	She wore **striped** socks.	Mary **quietly** read her book.

Mom knitted my **blue** sweater.	He created a **cool** robot.	He threw the ball **well**.
She read a **good** book.	He painted **perfectly**.	She ate **chocolate** ice cream.
He wrapped the **big** gifts.	She worked **hard**.	They typed **quickly**.

Color in the space if the boldfaced word is an adverb. Try to get three in a row.

He ran **fast**.	He **quickly** shoveled the snow.	She typed the paper **perfectly**.
Sonja **carefully** turned the page.	Jason waited **patiently**.	We went to **Michael's** house.
It was a **good** movie.	Sherry made **delicious** cookies.	Karen had a **timid** cat.

He ate a **cold** sandwich.	Mom bought the **blue** plates.	The **fat** caterpillar crawled.
Mom asked me **politely**.	She swam **faster** than last time.	Mrs. Karls played **wonder-fully**.
He colored the picture **neatly**.	Geralin picked the **yellow** flower.	She **sang** well last night.

Traits of Good Writing • 4–5 © 2004 Creative Teaching Press

Name _____ Date _____

In the Cafeteria

ADVERBS

An **adverb** describes the verb. Some adverbs tell when or where the action took place.

Underline the adverb in each sentence.

1 I woke up late today so I had to hurry.

2 Andrew sat next to Joseph.

3 Mrs. Parish walked around the lunchroom.

4 We will eat tacos for hot lunch tomorrow.

5 Alisha ate her dessert after her sandwich.

6 Conlan cleared the tables before recess.

7 He threw away his milk carton after he smashed it.

8 The principal stood nearby for the entire lunch hour.

9 Pete always uses a napkin when he eats spaghetti.

10 Kelly eats hot lunch today and so does Devin.

11 The handle on my lunch box broke today.

12 Frannie left her lunch money at home.

Traits of Good Writing • 4–5 © 2004 Creative Teaching Press

Name _____ Date _____

Outer Space

Adverbs

> An **adverb** is a word that describes a verb. Some adverbs tell how an action happened.

Underline the verb in each sentence. Circle the adverb and write it on the blank lines.

1 The earth is perfectly placed in the universe.

__ __ __ __ __ __ __ __
  1   2 3

2 The earth slowly rotates on its axis.

__ __ __ __ __ __
4 5 6

3 Marcus waited patiently for his turn
at the telescope.

__ __ __ __ __ __ __ __
   7   8

4 He quietly stared at the craters on the moon. _____

5 When the moon is exactly lined up with
the sun, it's called an equinox. _____

6 The astronaut carefully studied his information. _____

7 The stars shone brightly in the sky. _____

8 Jared cautiously climbed into the space ship. _____

9 She saw clearly through the telescope. _____

10 He suddenly noticed a meteorite in the sky. _____

11 The planets travel continuously around the sun. _____

12 The astronaut tightly fastened the seat belt. _____

Break the code by writing the numbered letters from above.

The word *astronaut* comes from two Greek root words meaning:

__ __ __ __   __ __ __ __ __ __
4 2 7 1   4 7 8 5 6 1

Traits of Good Writing • 4–5 © 2004 Creative Teaching Press

Letter of Complaint

CONTRACTIONS

Read the letter. Replace each pair of underlined words with a contraction from the word bank.

we're	didn't	you'll	isn't	can't	it's
doesn't	can't	doesn't	its	you'll	

Dear Toy Company,

    I bought a radio-controlled car last week. <u>It is</u> model number 2719. It <u>does</u>

<u>not</u> work. We followed the directions, but we still <u>can not</u> get it to work right.

We <u>did not</u> make a mistake. My dad and I tried everything, but it just <u>is not</u>

working. When you push the lever to the right, it goes backward. It <u>does not</u> go

forward at all. We <u>can not</u> figure it out. <u>We are</u> disappointed. We think <u>it is</u>

defective. We hope <u>you will</u> send us a new car. Our receipt is enclosed. We hope

<u>you will</u> honor our request.

                                     Thank you,

                                     Jared Jones

Traits of Good Writing • 4–5 © 2004 Creative Teaching Press

Name _____ Date _____

Our Soccer Team

Using Pronouns

A **pronoun** is a word used instead of a noun to refer to a person, place, or thing without naming it.
Examples: he, she, we, they

Read the sentences. Cross out the noun in the subject of each sentence. Replace it with a pronoun that could take the noun's place.

1 Robyn played a great game.

2 Jason hoped the game would never end.

3 Our team thinks the Panthers will surely win.

4 Justin scored a goal.

5 The boys and girls on that team were talented.

6 The goalie stopped several balls.

7 Their defenders were aggressive.

8 Sheila loves soccer more than any other sport.

9 The girl in the blue shorts was good.

10 The whole team had a great time.

11 The boys and girls can't wait to play that team next year.

12 My dad brought soda for the team to drink after the game.

Name _____ Date _____

Pool Party

HOMOPHONES

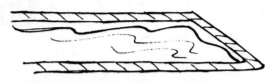

> **Homophones** are words that sound the same but have different spellings and meanings.
> Examples: too, to, two
> their, there, they're
> your, you're
> who's, whose

Circle the homophone that correctly completes each sentence.

Its/It's time for the first annual swimming pool party at Lion's Park in Mazomanie. Your/You're invited to come for some fun in the sun. Don't be two/to/too late in signing up or you'll/yule miss a good time. The pool will be open from to/two/too until four. Its/It's a perfect day for your/you're family to spend time together.

They're/Their/There will be concessions at the food stand and all T-shirts will sell for to/two/too dollars. Can you guess whose/who's going to be the surprise guest of honor? Your/You're right. Its/It's Mayor Doyle. He'll be they're/their/there in his swim trunks and goggles. It's/Its bound to be a great time for the entire town. We hope too/to/two see you their/they're/there.

Write the correct word next to its definition.

there, they're, their

A place   _____

Shows ownership   _____

Contraction of "they are"   _____

to, two, too

Going to a place   _____

A number   _____

Means "also"   _____

it's, its

Contraction of "it is"   _____

Means "belonging
to someone"   _____

who's, whose

Shows ownership   _____

Contraction of
"who is" or "who has"   _____

Traits of Good Writing • 4–5 © 2004 Creative Teaching Press

Name _____ Date _____

The Garden Snail

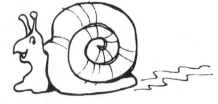

ACTION VERBS AND LINKING VERBS

The **action verbs** tell what snails **do**.
The **linking verbs** link the subject with words that tell what the snail **is like**. Some linking verbs are *am*, *is*, *are*, *was*, *were*, *become*, and *seem*.

Read the report about garden snails. Look for each verb. If it's a linking verb, circle it. If it's an action verb, underline it.

The garden snail is an interesting creature. It spends most of its day inside its shell. At night it comes out of its shell and feeds. Most garden snails eat leaves or plants. Some garden snails are carnivorous. They eat small insects and other snails. The snail's body can become 3 to 4 inches long. Garden snails produce a frothy substance as a form of defense.

Snails move by gliding on their flat, muscular foot. All snails are hermaphrodites. That means they can produce sperm and lay eggs. The snail hibernates with a large number of other snails. During long, hot, dry summers, the snails are inactive. The garden snail can live up to ten years.

There are 80,000 different species of snails in the world. The garden snail's shell is brown, flecked with black. The brown-lipped snail is brown, pink, or yellow. The two snails are hard to tell apart. Snails are edible. They are a delicacy to many people.

 Draw a picture of a snail on another sheet of paper. Write a poem about the snail. Use linking verbs and action verbs in your poem.

Car Wash

Main Verbs and Helping Verbs

Underline the main verb and circle the helping verb in each sentence. Then list each verb under the correct heading in the chart. Examples of helping verbs: is, am, are, was, can, have, may.

1 Justin was carrying the hose.

2 She is scrubbing the tires.

3 We are spraying the vehicle.

4 The kids have come to help.

5 They are working hard.

6 They may wash cars all day long.

7 Sandra is filling the buckets with water.

8 Mia is rinsing each soapy car.

9 Micah is getting wetter by the minute.

10 We may earn enough money for the trip.

11 Joseph is spraying Sophie with the hose.

12 Everyone was having fun.

Helping Verbs	Main Verbs

Traits of Good Writing • 4–5 © 2004 Creative Teaching Press

Name _____ Date _____

Computer Fun

CONJUNCTIONS

A **compound sentence** is made up of two simple sentences joined by a comma and followed by a conjunction such as *and*, *but*, or *so*.

Circle the conjunction in each sentence and correctly insert the comma. The first one is done for you.

1 I enjoy working on the computer, (but) sometimes I need to get up and stretch.

2 I like to play computer games and sometimes I just like typing.

3 Everyone likes computer class but it always seems to go by too fast.

4 Our computer teacher is nice but sometimes he raises his voice if we don't listen.

5 Reba likes to work at the computer so she does that during free choice time.

6 I work on the computer at school and I use the computer encyclopedia at home.

7 We have a computer in our living room and my Dad has one in the office.

8 Dad bought a digital camera and he is learning how to load pictures onto the computer.

9 I like to take pictures but I don't always hold the camera still enough.

10 Our camera is old and doesn't work well so we bought a new digital camera.

11 We can store the pictures on a tiny disk or Dad can put each picture inside the computer hard drive.

12 We took a family photo and my mom printed it right at home.

13 Dad says the computer was a great invention but the digital camera is an amazing machine.

Make up two simple sentences about computers. Write them below. Then write a compound sentence by joining the two sentences with a conjunction and a comma.

_____   _____

_____

Traits of Good Writing • 4–5 © 2004 Creative Teaching Press

Name _____   Date _____

Raccoons

NOUNS AND VERBS

Read the research paper about raccoons. Determine if each boldfaced word is a noun or a verb, and then write each word beneath the correct heading in the chart.

Have you ever looked outside your **tent** to find a **raccoon** digging through your **cooler** or trash can? Raccoons are frequent visitors at campsites. In fact, they can **survive** in any number of habitats. Most raccoons live in the wild. But they don't mind being near humans. Some have even been found in towns and **cities**.

The raccoon is known by its striped **face** and ringed tail. Raccoons have been hunted and trapped for their **fur**. The raccoon is a curious, clever animal. It will **eat** almost anything. The raccoon will hunt as it **swims**, looking for crayfish, **frogs**, and turtles. The raccoon will **catch** mice and muskrats and will also eat nuts, **fruit**, bird eggs, insects, or food from your cooler or trash can.

The raccoon's Latin name is *lotor*, meaning *one who washes*. Raccoons pick up their food with their **hands** and put it in their mouth. Often, a raccoon will **dip** its food into water to **rinse** off any sand or grit before eating it. A raccoon's **fingers** are as flexible as the fingers on a monkey. Raccoons can **twist** open doorknobs and turn handles.

The raccoon leads a solitary life. It will often **fight** with its own family members or other raccoons. Raccoons are nocturnal, which means they are most active at night. They do not hibernate. In the winter, the raccoon **grows** a thick **coat** to keep warm. Raccoons are interesting mammals. They are cute and cuddly to look at, but they would not make good pets.

Nouns	Verbs

Traits of Good Writing • 4–5 © 2004 Creative Teaching Press

Name _____ Date _____

Packer Football

That, Which, Who

Circle the word that correctly completes each sentence.

1 Football is a game (that/which) requires strong offense and defense.

2 The Green Bay Packers, (which/that/who) some call "America's Team," are talented on both offense and defense.

3 Brett Farve, (who/which) is a very talented quarterback, throws passes that are above and beyond that of many other quarterbacks.

4 The last season (which/that) Brett Farve led the Packers to the Super Bowl was in 1996.

5 The year two thousand four was the last time (who/that) the Packers went to the national playoffs.

6 The Green Bay Packer team, (which/who/that) trains in Green Bay, Wisconsin, includes great players from all over the United States.

7 Curly Lambeau, (which/that/who) was another famous Green Bay Packer, played for the team long ago.

8 Lambeau Field, (which/that) is named after Curly Lambeau, is a fun place to visit.

9 The Packers, (who/that/which) are known for their great fan support, are a winning team in the eyes of many, even when they have a losing season.

10 Everyone enjoys going to a Packer game, (which/that) makes it almost impossible to get tickets.

11 Ahman Green, Reggie White, and Antonio Freeman, (which/who) were all talented players, will be remembered by the fans forever.

Traits of Good Writing • 4–5 © 2004 Creative Teaching Press

Name _____ Date _____

Picnic

REAL AND VERY

Real is an adjective and must describe a noun or pronoun. It means "actual."
Very is an adverb that means "extremely."

Circle the word that correctly completes each sentence.

1 Mrs. Marston took us on a real/very outdoor picnic for science class.

2 We learned some real/very interesting things.

3 We know that ants are real/very attracted to food, especially sweet things.

4 The ants crawled all over a real/very sweet slice of apple we left out.

5 We also learned that bees are real/very attracted to cans of sweet soda pop.

6 We had a real/very fun time on this science class picnic.

7 We got to eat real/very food as well as learn some interesting things.

8 Jennifer brought some real/very good cheese to share with the class.

9 Sarah's mom baked cookies with real/very chocolate chips inside.

10 Jacob said the cookies were very/real good.

11 We sliced a real/very big watermelon and ate the whole thing.

12 It was real/very good.

13 Everyone had a very/real good time.

14 Even some real/very creatures from nature joined in the fun.

15 That was the real/very best science class I've ever attended.

16 Our teacher is a very/real peach.

Traits of Good Writing • 4–5 © 2004 Creative Teaching Press

Answer Key

What Do You Know? (page 5)

Answers will vary.

Picture Perfect (page 6)

1. d   **2.** b   **3.** e
4. f   **5.** a   **6.** c

Experiences (page 7)

Answers will vary.

Let's Explore! (page 8)

Answers will vary.

Project Pet (page 9)

Care

Brush her fur
Give her food and water
Take her for a walk
Bathe once a week
Hold and hug her
Clean her cage
Clip her nails

Food

Carrots
Apple slices
Pellets
Hay
Grass

Activities

Squeaks and chatters
Chews on chew stick
Build a maze for her
Sleeps

Start a Story (page 10)

It was a crazy day in art class. — b, d, h

It was the best birthday surprise I ever had. — a, e, k

I never had so much fun on a rainy day. — f, i, m

This was going to be the best Saturday our family ever spent together. — l, o, q

My mom is usually the best cook in our family. — j, n, p

There's nothing better than getting a brand-new pet. — c, g, r

It's Time to Write (page 11)

1. E   **6.** E
2. N   **7.** N
3. E   **8.** E
4. E   **9.** N
5. N   **10.** E

Please Expand (page 12)

Answers will vary. Possible answers include:

1. The dog barked:

   When: This morning, the dog barked.

   Size or Color: This morning, the large, brown dog barked.

   Place: This morning, the large, brown dog barked in front of my neighbor's house.

   Name: This morning, the large, brown dog barked in front of the Smiths' house.

2. The man ate:

   When: In the afternoon, the man ate.

   Size or Color: In the afternoon, the thin man ate.

   Place: In the afternoon, the thin man ate at his favorite restaurant.

   Name: In the afternoon, the thin man ate at his favorite restaurant, Mama Mia.

3. The team played:

   When: Yesterday, the team played.

   Size or Color: Yesterday, the championship team played.

   Place: Yesterday, the championship team played at the Sports Arena.

   Name: Yesterday, the West Side Wolverines played at the Sports Arena.

What's the Topic? (page 13)

The following sentences should be circled:

1. A puppy makes a wonderful pet.
2. Fishing with a fishing guide is the best way to fish.
3. School is great!
4. My grandpa is a great guy.
5. Raccoons are interesting animals.
6. Ping-Pong™ is a great game.
7. Watching a professional basketball game is exciting.

Sentences will vary.

Parts of a Paragraph (page 14)

1. detail
  detail
  detail
  topic
  concluding

2. detail
  topic
  detail
  concluding
  detail

3. detail
  detail
  topic
  detail
  concluding

Sports (page 15)

Soccer
kick the ball
can't touch the ball
has a goalie
big ball

Both
play with one ball
wear a uniform
many players on a team

Baseball
wear a cap
catch the ball
throw the ball
wear a batting glove
wear spikes
small ball
uses an umpire
use a bat
use a glove

Healthy Me (page 16)

1. j
2. c
3. d
4. a
5. b
6. f
7. g
8. h
9. i
10. e

Fishbowl (page 17)

Answers may vary. Possible answer includes:
1. First, pour the fish and some of the water into a different container.
2. Then pour the rest of the dirty water down the drain.
3. Be careful not to let the pebbles fall into the drain.
4. Place a drop of dish liquid in the dirty bowl.
5. Then add warm water.
6. Next, wash and scrub the inside of the bowl, along with any shells, coral, or rocks with the soapy water.
7. After that, rinse everything several times until no more soap bubbles appear.
8. Then add fresh water to the clean bowl.
9. Let the fresh water stand until it's room temperature.
10. Finally, put the fish into the clean fishbowl.

In the Kitchen (page 18)

Pizza
Preheat oven to 400°
Unwrap pizza
Place pizza in the oven
Bake for 15 minutes
Remove pizza from the oven
Cut into slices and enjoy

Macaroni and Cheese
Pour noodles into a pan of boiling water
Boil noodles for 7 minutes
Drain noodles
Add butter, milk, and cheese sauce packet
Stir until well combined
Spoon into bowls and enjoy

Fun in the Sun (page 19)

Hiking
1. detail
2. main idea
3. detail
4. detail
5. irrelevant
6. detail
7. detail
8. detail

The Water Park
1. detail
2. detail
3. detail
4. main idea
5. detail
6. detail
7. irrelevant
8. detail
9. detail

A Trip to the Library (page 20)

1. yes
2. no
3. yes
4. no
5. yes
6. no
7. no
8. yes
9. no
10. no
11. yes
12. no
13. no
14. yes
15. no
16. yes
17. yes
18. yes
19. no
20. yes

Story Parts (page 21)

1. B
2. E
3. M
4. B
5. E
6. B
7. M
8. E
9. B
10. E
11. B
12. E
13. B
14. E

Life Story (page 22)

Sports and Hobbies
Won the fifty-yard freestyle race
Caught a 6-inch Walleye Pike
Joined the Cub Scouts
Hit a home run in a little league game

School
Made many new friends.
Mrs. Jones was my third grade teacher.
I got my first A in math class.
Visited the museum for a field trip

Family
We moved from Alabama to Wisconsin
My dad bought a new puppy.
My baby brother, Jake, was born.
Vacationed in California

A Can of Critters (page 23)

1. Melanie
2. Melanie's grandfather's house; Melanie's room
3. Melanie finds some new pets.
4. Melanie wants to keep the pets hidden from her mother.
5. She hides the pets but they get loose.
6. Melanie's mom discovers the pets.
7. Melanie is in trouble and she decides to let the pets go.

Attention Please! (page 24)

The following sentences should be circled:

It was an awesome lollipop.

How do you like a juicy footlong, fresh off the grill?
Ketchup and mustard? Pickles and onion?

I sat by the lake minding my own business, when a loud
flapping noise nearly scared me half to death.

Let's End Well (page 25)

1. star	6. sad face	11. sad face
2. sad face	7. sad face	12. star
3. star	8. star	13. sad face
4. sad face	9. star	14. star
5. star	10. star	

Smooth Transitions (page 26)

addition	also	additionally	furthermore
comparison	in the same way	likewise	equally
example	a case in point	to illustrate	for instance
result	consequently	hence	therefore
summary/ conclusion	in brief	finally	in the end

Sequence a Story (page 27)

Michael's Birthday
First
Introduction
Conclusion
Second
Third

Marcus Saves the Day
Conclusion
First
Second
Introduction
Third

Lucas' Science Project
First
Second
Third
Introduction
Conclusion

In the Doghouse (page 28)

Have you ever climbed through a doghouse on your hands and knees at 6:30 in the morning, with the dog inside? I did. It all began one morning when my family was eating breakfast. We were just about to clear the table when there was a knock at the door. Who would be here at this early hour? my mother wondered. I wondered the same thing.

① When my dad opened the door, there stood Mr. Carlson in his pajamas. I was about to laugh when I heard him say, "I'm locked out of my house. Could one of your girls come over and help me out? I need someone small who can fit inside the doghouse entrance. Then we can get into the garage where there's a key and I can get inside." Unfortunately, I'm the smallest person in the family, so I was nominated for the job.

② Dad and I walked over to Mr. Carlson's backyard. I opened the miniature door to the doghouse and wriggled my way through. It wasn't easy. "Here Chester, it's OK," I called nervously, as I looked him in the eye. He was happy to see me. However, I couldn't say the same. I crept along on my hands and knees with Chester close behind me sniffing all the way.

③ After several uncomfortable seconds, I made it through the small opening into the garage. Mr. Carlson told me where the key was, and ④ I opened the house up for him. I bet he was glad to get inside and change into his clothes.

⑤ He thanked me several times. Later that day, Mr. Carlson brought me a package of candy and a small toy for a reward. I thought that was great. Dad said he appreciated my helpful attitude. I was just glad it was over. Dogs and dog cages are not my idea of a fun way to start the day.

Crossword Fun (page 29)

Across

4. conclusion
5. climax
7. conflict
8. plot

Down

1. beginning
2. middle
3. end
4. characters
6. setting

What Is Voice? (page 30)

1. care
2. expression
3. person
4. unique
5. feelings
6. voice

Take Me Out to the Ball Game (page 31)

The following sentences should be underlined:

It was great how our team came from behind and won the championship game by two runs.

The fans were on the edge of their seats.

Everyone jumped up and cheered when Johnny struck out the last batter.

The fans went wild and so did I.

There's nothing better than beating a tough team like the Tigers.

The players lifted Johnny into the air and we carried him around the field.

The crowd roared and stomped their feet.

It was the best game we ever played.

When I rounded third base, my cap flew off but I didn't stop running.

The following sentences should be crossed out:

We played baseball.

We won the game.

People thought we might lose.

Johnny is a good pitcher.

It was a nice baseball game.

Our team had fun.

The team was glad to win.

We were happy.

Everyone was happy we won.

The team was glad to win.

It was a nice game.

I knew I would make it home.

It's nice to win.

It was a good baseball game.

Learning About Voice (page 32)

The following list indicates whether the sentence should be circled or crossed out:

1. circle
2. cross out
3. circle
4. circle
5. circle
6. circle
7. cross out
8. circle
9. cross out
10. circle
11. cross out
12. circle
13. circle

The Zoo (page 33)

The following sentences should be underlined:

I'd never been to the zoo in the middle of the night before.

It seemed unusually quiet and especially dark that night.

I wonder what the reptiles thought of all of us kids sleeping in their building.

Jamie and I curled up in our sleeping bags beneath the iguana display.

I wondered how many pairs of reptile eyes were watching me sleep.

It was weird to hear the tortoises crawling around in the dark.

Cages of reptiles surrounded us.

When Jamie said, "We might wake up face-to-face with a boa," I was shaking in my sleeping bag.

It was the most exciting sleepover I've ever been to.

The following sentences should be crossed out:

We slept at the zoo.

We walked in at night.

We brought sleeping bags.

There were reptiles.

We liked sleeping there.

It was a nice sleepover.

Coach (page 34)

My basketball coach is Todd Barsness. He is a really good coach. He coaches well. He knows a lot about basketball. He tells us what to do. He's nice. I like having him for a coach.

I wouldn't trade Coach Barsness for the world. He's the best in the 5th grade conference. All the kids on the team say he's an awesome coach, and they mean it. He's taught our team so many new basketball skills. Coach Barsness said we're "all going to play like Michael Jordan someday." I can already see that I'm playing a lot better than last year.

Coach Barsness is tough, too. He really works the team hard. There's no easy practice or slacking off with him around. Everyone shoots thirty free throws before practice even begins, and running ten sets of line-grabbers is a part of our daily training. Coach says, "That's how we will build a strong team."

He also teaches us about good sportsmanship, respecting our teammates, and obeying the coach's orders. When you make a mistake during a game he pulls you aside and puts his hand on your shoulder. He says, "Do you know what happened out there? Then don't worry about it." Then later on he tells us how to improve.

Coach Barsness has developed a strong team of basketball players this year. If we win the conference championship, we owe it all to him.

Dialogue (page 35)

A cat is the best pet ever.
Not for me. I love snakes.
Snakes? Why snakes?
Because they love you back.

I wish we could ride our bikes to school.
Yeah, the bus ride is always so long—45 minutes of boredom.
Oh, no! Flat tire.
Maybe 45 minutes wasn't so bad after all.

First or Third? (page 36)

1. third	4. first	7. first	10. third
2. first	5. first	8. third	11. third
3. third	6. third	9. first	12. first

Persuade Me (page 37)

The following statements should be circled:
2,3,5,7,9,10,11,13,14

A Treat for the Reader (page 38)

1. dreary	6. frigid	10. dashed
2. frolicked	7. cozy	11. devoured
3. shattered	8. whispered	12. hurled
4. spied	9. slithered	13. tossed
5. chuckled		

Said	Went	Looked
declared	trotted	observed
exclaimed	tiptoed	spied
announced	crept	spotted
shouted	danced	studied

Be Specific (page 39)

Answers will vary. Possible answers include:
1. I put on my galoshes to go out in the rain.
2. My father drove me in his Corvette to Johnny's Famous Deli.
3. I saw a black and white Dalmation in the window of the pet store.
4. We ate juicy hamburgers and crispy fries for lunch.
5. I had a delicious chocolate and vanilla swirled cheesecake for dessert.
6. We went into the mansion.
7. I wore a red beret.
8. My sister can speak both Spanish and French.

A Secret Message (page 40)

1. determine	8. constructed
2. creating	9. whispered
3. skipped	10. hike
4. glared	11. earn
5. won	12. pranced
6. observed	13. zoomed
7. declared	

The Robot (page 41)

Answers will vary.

1. discovered	9. attached
2. studied	10. glued
3. created	11. shouted
4. gathered	12. ran
5. constructed	13. hurried
6. formed	14. admired
7. drew	15. declared
8. inserted	16. exclaimed

Adding Adjectives (page 42)

1. brown leather	5. leather basketball
2. floppy maroon	6. gooey and sticky
3. ice cold	7. six fuzzy
4. hot crackling	8. huge beige

9–13. Answers will vary.

Antonym Search (page 43)

Across	Down
1. bloom	2. imaginary
3. repaired	5. tactful
4. reject	7. local
6. refreshed	9. achieve
8. capable	12. weakened
10. hastily	14. undependable
11. vague	
13. suddenly	

Sunflower Fun (page 44)

1. festive	7. dishonest
2. introduce	8. excess
3. create	9. barren
4. compromise	10. convince
5. amateur	11. eager
6. first	12. reliable

Get Happy with Homonyms (page 45)

1. hour	8. cent
2. clothes	9. course
3. we'd	10. waist
4. would	11. peace
5. whole	12. weather
6. allowed	13. through
7. peer	

Same or Opposite (page 46)

1. A	5. A	9. S	13. S
2. S	6. A	10. A	14. S
3. S	7. S	11. S	15. A
4. S	8. S	12. A	16. S

Comparisons (page 47)

Answers will vary. Possible answers include:

1. cheetah
2. skyscraper
3. hog
4. bird
5. fox
6. picture
7. lark
8. wink
9. silk
10. button
11. bat
12. molasses
13. fox
14. mouse

Write a Postcard (page 48)

Dear Laura,

I'm sending this postcard from the Milwaukee Museum. It's interesting. It's a nice place to go. You would like it. See you soon.

Anna

Dear Abigail,

The Milwaukee Museum is a wonderful place to visit. I'm learning so much about many topics. There's a great display on ancient Egypt. We even saw a real mummy.

We also visited an old town from the early nineteen hundreds and got to buy candy at the General Store. Then we saw a huge display about dinosaurs. We climbed inside the skeleton of a brontosaurus. We ate cheeseburgers for lunch in the cafeteria.

You would have loved the butterfly exhibit. You can walk through a beautiful garden setting and there are literally hundreds of butterflies in all different shapes, sizes, and colors. A pretty orange monarch butterfly landed on my shoulder.

I hope you and I can visit the museum together sometime this summer.

Your friend,
Anna

Colorful Captions (page 49)

Answers will vary.

Diamante Poem (page 50)

Answers will vary.

Persuasive or Not (page 51)

1. P
2. N
3. P
4. P
5. P
6. N
7. P
8. P
9. P
10. N
11. P

Active vs. Passive (page 52)

1. The bee stung the boy.
2. Scientists conducted experiments to test the hypothesis.
3. My father washed the car.
4. The teacher taught the students.
5. The comedian told several jokes.
6. All fourth-graders will learn science and math.
7. Tom will report the news at 5:00 p.m.
8. The school secretary answered the phone.

Adventures in Alliteration (page 53)

1. Rex and Randi ran right down Ranger Road in the rain.
2. Bob Baxter bought a big black bat for baseball.
3. Thomas taught Tess to tap her toes on Tuesday.
4. Seventy sailors sang silly songs by the sea.
5. Fred feasted on french fries and fish the first Friday in February.

Sentences will vary.

Assonance Examples (page 54)

The following phrases should be circled:

Sue's blue shoes
Keating Street
Wade makes mistakes.
Sleep beneath the trees.
Eat green beans.
Vince isn't in.
in the tin bin
high as a kite
Joy pointed at the boys.
Ray paid for Jane.

flying high
Pet the red hen.
She reads.
Shane makes mistakes.
The boys enjoyed the toys.
five kind guys
Winnie isn't fishing.
Eat at Pete's.
wise guys
rapid traffic

Weak or Strong? (page 55)

The following sentences should be circled:

Ahhhh, there's nothing like the sights and sounds and smells of the carnival.

James didn't mind that the path was leaf-covered, dusty, and not very wide at all, for he was too busy thinking about Bastion.

The crock of chili was piping hot, and the smell of the freshly baked yeast rolls made my mouth water.

The slippery, slimy creature slipped right out of my hands, so I grabbed it by the legs and then held on tightly.

There's nothing better than getting dirty and digging and planting in the sweet-smelling, rich, black soil.

For the three of us, biking is a time of talking, coasting, popping wheelies, and just riding around hanging out together.

Know the Characters (page 56)

Answers will vary. Possible answers include:

1. talk — Sammy is an honest person.
2. talk — Sarah is not considerate of others' feelings.
3. act — Jamie is a nice and considerate person.
4. talk — Trish is friendly.
5. look — Mr. Iverson is upset.
6. look — The girl is cute and looks like a doll.
7. talk — Polly is a perfectionist and conceited.
8. think — Jackson is self-confident.

Used Very Much (page 57)

Answers will vary. Possible answers include:

1. It was an incredibly hot day.
2. The car moved particularly slowly.
3. Karen is remarkably intelligent.
4. Derek runs amazingly fast.
5. The shopping bag is exceedingly full.
6. The grasshopper jumps exceptionally high.
7. The movie was awfully scary.
8. She parked the car really close to the curb.
9. The bell rang extraordinarily loudly.
10. I am extremely tired.

Cinquain Poetry (page 58)

The following poems should be circled:

　Basketball and Bedroom

Cookies
Tasty crunchy
Bake Eat Enjoy
Packed with chocolate chunks
Dessert

Having Fun with Idioms (page 59)

1. d	4. l	7. h	10. b
2. e	5. j	8. i	11. c
3. f	6. g	9. k	12. a

Bug Off (page 60)

1. heads — b	5. worked — g	9. edge — e
2. hands — j	6. bit — h	10. leg — f
3. death — d	7. cut — i	11. hit — l
4. cats — a	8. splash — k	12. off — c

In Other Words (page 61)

1. repairman	5. dad	9. teacher
2. uncle	6. actor	10. salesman
3. postman	7. doctor	11. reporter
4. brother	8. scientist	12. fireman

Baseball (page 62)

Answers may vary. Possible answers include:

See: beautiful, colorful blankets, brother, players, diamond

Hear: National Anthem, introduced players, snap of bat pierced air, noon whistle, cheered and clapped, coaches barking out orders, OUTTT

Smell: popcorn, hot dogs

Taste: ketchup, mustard, cola, hot dog, sweet flavor, bubble gum

Touch or Feel: breezy, excitement, ice cold, refreshing, hot summer day, quenched thirst, sun, scorching sun, calm nerves, chewed wildly, crushed can

Gym Class (page 63)

Answers will vary.

Moving Day (page 64)

sit — sat	didn't — don't
has — have	does — did
didn't — doesn't	sit — sat
watch — watched	unpack — unpacked
does — do	hear — heard
reply — replied	jumps — jumped
was — were	exclaim — exclaimed
doesn't — didn't	were — was
wondered — wonder	hang — hung
was — is	wouldn't — won't
had — having	race — raced

Hidden message: Make new friends.

All Together Now (page 65)

Answers will vary.

At the Pond (page 66)

1. (Jason) caught six toads.
2. (Tanya) picked up a turtle and watched it crawl in the sand.
3. (Hallie) found a caterpillar with brown and black fur.
4. (They) will fall in if they walk on those rocks.
5. (Mom) caught minnows with a small net.
6. (I) picked up litter and threw it away.
7. (Dad) skipped stones on the water.
8. (Hudson) found a fishing lure and gave it to me.
9. Did (Reba) throw away the can after she drank her soda?
10. (She) watched the geese fly in a V formation.
11. Did (Bryce) scare the ducks away?
12. (I) can't believe you did that!

Sentence or Fragment (page 67)

1. F
2. S
3. S
4. F
5. F
6. S
7. S
8. F
9. S
10. F
11. F
12. F
13. S
14. S
15. F
16. F
17. S
18. S

Make It Complete (page 68)

Answers will vary.

Better Beginnings (page 69)

Art Class

Art class
Students
My favorite
I look forward
It's fun

Sentences will vary.

Bananas

Bananas are
They go
I eat
They make
This fabulous fruit

Sentences will vary.

Compound It (page 70)

The following sentences should be circled:

2. Miah went to the store, and then she stopped at the pharmacy.
4. Devin went to the theatre, and then he and his dad ate at McDonald's.
5. She wants to go to the mall for her birthday, or she wants to have friends over.
6. Justin likes bowling, but he thinks soccer is more fun.
7. Casey has a dog, but she says she would rather have a kitten for a pet.
8. Joylin ordered a hamburger and her mom ordered a vanilla milk shake.
10. Micah and Zach rode their bikes to the park, but they forgot to stop at the post office to mail the letter.
11. Jose and Darwin had been best friends since preschool, but now they each have new best friends.

Spiders (page 71)

Answers will vary. Possible answers include:

1. Spiders have eight legs and two body parts.
2. Spiders are helpful because they eat insects.
3. There are many kinds of spiders, but not all kinds live in the United States.
4. Shelley couldn't get to sleep because she saw a spider on the ceiling in her bedroom.
5. Spiders make great pets, although spiders sometimes scare people.
6. One common spider is called daddy long legs because it has very long legs.
7. Justin caught a spider for a pet, but his mother would not let him keep it.
8. The spider didn't survive in the jar because it didn't have food or enough air.
9. A spider will tickle you, although you have to let it crawl on your arm first.
10. Spiders live outdoors and inside your home.
11. People think cobwebs come from spiders, but they are simply made from dust gathering in your home.

Stretch It Out (page 72)

Answers will vary.

Birthday Fun (page 73)

1. because
2. or
3. and
4. before
5. and
6. although
7. but
8. because
9. but
10. and
11. because

Bowling (page 74)

The following phrases and sentences should be crossed out:
Bowling is great.
It's great to bowl with friends.
We're going to Florida this summer.
Fifth graders should use an eight-pound ball.
You can use the bowling shoes that are there.
My friend Matt is sleeping over this weekend.
The French fries are hot.
The juice is cold.
We laugh a lot when we bowl.
I'd rather bowl than watch cartoons on Saturdays.

At the Restaurant (page 75)

1. fifteen long
2. long wooden
3. cheerful
4. hot ham
5. lemon iced
6. tall plastic
7. chocolate
8. ice cold
9. Chinese chicken
10. grilled cheese
11. fancy ice cream
12. best
13. fanciest
14. generous

Ice Cream (page 76)

1. declarative
2. declarative
3. exclamatory
4. imperative
5. declarative
6. exclamatory
7. interrogative
8. declarative
9. imperative
10. declarative
11. declarative
12. interrogative

Cousins (page 77)

Dear Gibson,

How are you doing? I haven't heard from you in a long time. Write to me. How is your family? We're doing fine in Wisconsin. Spring is here and it's a lot warmer now. Everyone is wearing shorts to school because it's sixty degrees. I can't wait for summer! You have to see my new skateboard. It's the coolest! I'm getting pretty good at riding it. Buy one! You'll love riding it after school each day.

Next week we have spring break. I can't wait! We're going to a movie on Monday and then out for pizza. On Friday my dad is off from work so we'll do something together like fishing or hiking. How about you? When do you have spring break?

Last week we started soccer practice. Our first game will be next weekend. Soccer is the coolest sport!

I'm looking forward to seeing you at the family reunion this summer. I hope we get to go boating and fishing again this year. I knew I'd catch a bigger fish than you! Have fun!

Write back.

Thomas

Dear Thomas,

I bet I can outfish you this year. I have a new pole and some great new tackle. Not much is going on around here. We had spring break last week. It was fun. It was great to sleep late every day. We visited Grandma. She's doing well. Write to her. She misses seeing you.

I rode on a skateboard once. No thanks! I had more bandages on my knees and legs than you could count. I'll stick to biking. My dad bought a new seat and shock absorbers for my bike. I love riding over the hills in the field and jumping over the ramps we built last summer.

Say hi to your family. See you at the reunion. The fishing contest begins at 6:00 a.m. that Saturday morning. Be ready!

Gibson

Let's Go to the Movies (page 78)

1. Find a seat where we can see.
2. Go to the movie before supper.
3. Keep your eyes on the screen.
4. Eat your popcorn before the movie starts.
5. Sit close to the center of the theater.
6. Don't spill your soda.
7. Wait here.
8. Buy the tickets.
9. Don't be afraid.
10. Get comfortable in your chair.
11. Enjoy the previews before the show.

Happy Holidays (page 79)

1. January
2. Thanksgiving
3. Halloween
4. Presidents' Day
5. Valentine's Day
6. Independence Day
7. November
8. December
9. New Year's Day
10. April Fool's Day
11. July
12. February
13. August

My Favorites (page 80)

Favorite Cereals and Snack Foods
Froot Loops
Frosted Flakes
Snickers

Favorite Books and Movies
Runaway Ralph
Holes
Parent Trap
Star Wars
Harry Potter

Favorite Cities and Places to Visit
Chicago
San Diego Zoo

Favorite Restaurants
Pizza Hut
Burger King
McDonald's

Favorite Sports Teams
Green Bay Packers
Seattle Seahawks
New York Yankees
Los Angeles Lakers

School Rules (page 81)

The following words are misspelled and should be circled:

1. buble (bubble)
2. showt (shout), lowd (loud), quizz (quiz)
3. snax (snacks), krackers (crackers)
4. teecher (teacher), raize (raise), studunt (student)
5. pilows (pillows), tried (tired)
6. lounnge (lounge)
7. seeting (seating), arraingement (arrangement)
8. relacks (relax), finnish (finish), there (their)
9. muzic (music)
10. therty (thirty), reces (recess), our (hour)
11. berthday (birthday), piza (pizza),
12. frends (friends)

What's That Buzz? (page 82)

1. "This is a great day for a walk through the field," declared Greg.
2. "It's nice of your parents to take us on a hike," added Jose.
3. "Yeah, my parents are pretty cool," replied Greg.
4. Marcie said, "Look out for that beehive. It's huge."
5. "I hate bees!" replied Jose.
6. "Me too," exclaimed Greg. "I remember when my little brother got stung. He cried for a long time."
7. "I bet it hurts a lot," answered Marcie.
8. "My mom says they won't bother you, if you don't bother them," replied Jose.
9. Greg's mom smiled and whispered, "I remember when two bees stung your dad."
10. "Don't remind me!" exclaimed Dad.
11. "I think I'll stand over here," declared Greg.
12. "Me too!" exclaimed Jose.

School Days (page 83)

1. Are you buying a hot or cold lunch today?
2. Sarah didn't finish her homework.
3. Wow! That was the hardest test I've ever taken.
4. Sheila's locker couldn't open.
5. Can we call Mr. Marx to help open the locker?
6. Who is you teacher this year?
7. Fire drill, everybody line up!
8. Would you like to play soccer at recess?
9. Art class is my favorite time of day. How about you?
10. What time is recess?
11. The bus ride was too long.
12. Do you want milk or juice?
13. Stephanie and Miles think gym class is the best.
14. What is the new music teacher's name?

Pet Guinea Pig (page 84)

1. Guinea pigs are excellent pets; they require very little time and attention.
2. Caring for a guinea pig is very simple; you just have to feed it, hold it, and love it.
3. Guinea pigs enjoy attention; they love being held and caressed.
4. Guinea pigs like to hide under some kind of shelter; a shoe box, a plastic container, or a store-bought, wooden bridge are all good choices.
5. Sometimes your pet will give a sign that it wants your attention; he or she will squeak when you enter the room.
6. A guinea pig's diet is very simple; all it requires are carrots, grass or hay, and guinea pig pellets.
7. Their habitat is easy to manage; just change the cedar shavings in their cage once a week.
8. Guinea pigs are quiet animals most of the time; they sit and relax in their cage for much of the day.
9. Guinea pigs also enjoy various activities; they like walking outdoors, running around the house, and chewing on chew sticks.
10. Guinea pigs are contented animals; they are happy to be alone, with people, or with other friendly guinea pigs.
11. A carrot is a favorite treat for most guinea pigs; just place one in the cage, and they'll eat it right away.

Careful with Commas (page 85)

1. Andy, Drew, and Joe came over after school.
2. The boys hung up their coats, hats, and backpacks.
3. Joe did his chores, and Drew and Andy helped.
4. We played soccer, baseball, and checkers.
5. We ate crackers, cheese, and popcorn for a snack.
6. We passed, dribbled, and dunked the basketball.
7. "Boys, time to come in for supper," called Mrs. Murray.
8. "Okay, we're coming," replied Joe.
9. Joe's mom served pizza, carrots, and garlic bread for supper.
10. Drew did his math homework, and Andy and Joe finished the science project.
11. "Yes, we'd like to come over tomorrow, too," declared Andy and Drew.
12. Joe showed his rock collection to Andy, and Drew looked at Joe's robot collection.

At the Beach (page 86)

1. Jennifer's swimsuit has red and white stripes.
2. We're all going for a swim.
3. Mom's sun hat has pink flowers all over it.
4. Jacob's sand castle had a flag on top.
5. She's going to float on an air mattress.
6. Dad's blowing up the inner tube.
7. I sat on my dad's towel.
8. He's practicing the backstroke.
9. We're all putting on sunscreen.
10. We didn't have trouble finding Olbrich Beach.
11. We're going to eat lunch in the shade.
12. They're carrying the blanket and basket over there.
13. There were sand pails and shovels on all the children's towels.
14. The sand was in my brother's hair and his swimsuit.
15. Josiah wore Mom's sunglasses.

Pen Pal (page 87)

The following are the corrected words to insert:

doing	thought	skateboard	fun
heard	chicken	birthday	office
doing	great	November	farther
school	played	have	usual
country	Saturday	skateboards	does
there	anyway	better	hope
restaurant	remember	driveway	write

Shelley's Spelling List (page 88)

1. education
2. continent
3. energy
4. gravity
5. blizzard
6. attic
7. behind
8. paragraph
9. mayor
10. important
11. piece
12. slippery
13. receive
14. allow
15. reason
16. frightened

Message:
Spelling is fun!

Lunchtime (page 89)

1. The chocolate milk is very cold.
2. This Granny Smith apple is crunchy and sour.
3. My cherry juice box spilled all over the table.
4. I like tuna sandwiches with lettuce on top.
5. I ate my chocolate cupcake before my sandwich.
6. Mom packed carrots and dip in my lunch.
7. Strawberry-banana yogurt is one of my favorites.
8. Crunchy corn chips are the best part of lunchtime.
9. Peanut butter sandwiches are always good with jelly or bananas.
10. The granola bar was apple flavored.
11. I stacked sliced cheese on my saltine crackers.
12. The turkey sandwich was great on rye bread.

Spaghetti Is Best (page 90)

The following are simple subjects:

2. Parmesan cheese is a tasty topping to sprinkle on the spaghetti.
3. My mom makes the best spaghetti in the world.
4. My family usually eats spaghetti on Wednesday nights.
5. My older brother would eat spaghetti every day if my parents would let him.
6. My little sister always gets sauce on her face and in her hair.
7. The meatballs are my favorite part.
8. My dad usually ends up getting sauce on his shirt.
9. Hot, buttery garlic bread is another food that goes great with spaghetti.
10. My mom says I must be part Italian.
11. The slippery long noodles are fun to twirl on your fork.

Pizza Party (page 91)

1. Matthew loves pepperoni pizza.
2. My family eats at the Pizza Plaza almost every week.
3. Jordan says olives are his favorite topping.
4. Jacqueline discovered a new pizza place at the mall.
5. We travel to the Pizza Pit-Stop whenever we're in town.
6. My grandma orders pizza from Charlie's Diner.
7. Mr. Manning stopped for carryout pizza.
8. They built a new pizza restaurant on Maple Street.
9. The girls walked to the Pizza Palace.
10. Isaac and David bought a frozen pizza from Gander's Grocery.
11. My brother works at the Pizza Shop.
12. Barry and I order pizza for lunch sometimes.
13. My brother always gives my sister the biggest slice.

At the Carnival (page 92)

1. My whole family enjoyed the carnival.
2. The clown juggled five oranges at one time.
3. Jenny ate all her cotton candy.
4. My parents bought a large pizza.
5. I drank a tall glass of ice cold soda.
6. Jason and I played games on the midway.
7. Dad won a prize at the ring toss game
8. Mom and I rode three different rides together.
9. We watched a fireworks display at night.
10. Dad ordered footlong hot dogs for everyone.
11. My family spent twenty-five dollars at the carnival.

Bedroom Bonanza (page 93)

1. under the bed
2. on the floor
3. in the doorway
4. on the shelf
5. from the library
6. on the floor
7. in the garage
8. in the hamper
9. on the bed
10. on the table
11. on the closet floor
12. around the bedroom
13. under the toy shelf

Computer Match-Up (page 94)

1. A word that shows action — verb
2. A punctuation mark at the end of a question — question mark
3. A word that describes a verb — adverb
4. A person, place, thing, or idea — noun
5. A specific word that takes the place of a noun — proper noun
6. A word that describes a noun — adjective
7. The part of a sentence that tells who or what the sentence is about — subject
8. The part of a sentence that tells what the subject is or does — predicate
9. The noun or pronoun that receives the action of the verb — direct object
10. A sentence that gives an order — command
11. A sentence that shows strong feelings — exclamation
12. A word that joins two simple sentences together to make a compound sentence — conjunction

Yard Work (page 95)

Answers will vary. Possible answers include:

1. Mom raked up the grass and trimmed the bushes. She also picked up twigs.
2. Mr. Lord let us use his weed trimmer and two of his shovels. He showed us how to plant a tree.
3. James took off his jacket and helped his dad. He carried the trash bag and the tools.
4. I dug up the weeds and planted a bush. I also helped Mom plant tulips.
5. Dad wanted to mow the lawn and put down fertilizer. We picked up any litter we could find.
6. My sister helped rake the leaves and she brought out lemonade and cookies. She asked Dad if we were almost finished with the work.

In the City (page 96)

1. The stores are open early. It's a busy day in the city.
2. Many cars are stopped. The people honk their horns.
3. Many people cross the street. It's a busy corner.
4. It's noisy in the city. The dogs bark loudly.
5. The shoppers carry packages. They are having fun.
6. Two men walk into the restaurant. They're going to eat lunch.
7. The woman talks on her cell phone. She's on her way home.
8. Mr. James sweeps off the steps. He puts a sign in the window.
9. The boys walk on the sidewalk. Each one has a package.
10. Mrs. Murray has her dog on a leash. I hope it doesn't get away. It's a big dog.
11. The storeowner opened the shop. He let the people in early.
12. Shopping in the city is fun. It's a very busy place.
13. People on bikes wait to cross the road. They're all wearing helmets.
14. The officer helps direct traffic. Everyone goes around the construction workers.

At the Mall (page 97)

The following words should be circled:

1. those
2. this
3. these
4. that
5. those
6. this
7. this
8. these
9. this
10. this
11. these
12. this

Have fun shopping!

Just a Note (page 98)

Dear Mom,

Mimi called to see if I could **come** over. I **went** to her house to try her new computer game. I **have** my homework with me. I hope you **don't** mind that I'm **gone**.

Love, Sophie

Joe,

Do you **have** the book I **gave** you? I **came** over to borrow it, but you **were** gone. I **was** hoping you'd be home. Can I **come** over when you **get** home?

Toby

P.S. You **have** to see my new skateboard!

Mr. Boston,

We **have** your mail. The postman **gave** it to us when you **were** gone. We can **come** over when you **get** home.

The Murrays

Birthday Party (page 99)

Singular Nouns	Plural Nouns
party	friends
cake	kids
hat	presents
song	scoops
prize	games
house	favors
	notes

Person, Place, Thing, or Idea (page 100)

The following nouns should be circled:

1. Shelly (person), door (thing)
2. class (place), Justin (person), teacher (person), chair (thing)
3. Benjamin (person), gum (thing), class (place)
4. Mr. Kenny (person), teacher (person), whistle (thing)
5. Ms. Darst (person), pot (thing), example (idea), class (people)
6. songs (things), class (place)
7. sister (person), Sophia (person), book (thing), Holes (thing)
8. Trevor (person), backpack (thing), homework (thing)
9. Mr. Williams (person), locker (thing), Pledge of Allegiance (thing)
10. day (thing), school (place), events (thing)
11. games (things), tug-of-war (thing), water-balloon toss (thing)

Dear Uncle Dave (page 101)

Dear Uncle Dave,

I'm sorry you missed my soccer game. We beat the Tigers six to three. It was the coolest game ever. I scored two goals. My friend Alan scored two goals also. I ran as fast as I could and kicked the ball more than ever before. I played goalie, too. I was a good defender. My coach put me in all four quarters of the game. Mom and Dad laughed when I fell down. I laughed, too. I rested during half time. Boy, was I tired. Allie watched the game from her stroller. When the whistle blew at the end, I jumped up and down. Mom clapped. Dad threw his hat into the air. I cheered as loudly as I could. The whole team played a great game. I hope you can come to my next game.

Justin

Skates and Skateboards (page 102)

1. a	6. the	11. the
2. The	7. a	12. an
3. a	8. a	13. The
4. a	9. the	14. an
5. an	10. the	

Tic-Tac-Toe (page 103)

The **long** pencil broke.	The raccoon grew a **thick** coat.	She had **curly** hair.
He wore a **black** cap.	They jogged **together**.	We **quickly** folded the papers.
He listened **carefully**.	She wore **striped** socks.	Mary **quietly** read her book.

Mom knitted my **blue** sweater.	He created a **cool** robot.	He threw the ball **well**.
She read a **good** book.	He painted **perfectly**.	She ate **chocolate** ice cream.
He wrapped the **big** gifts.	She worked **hard**.	They typed **quickly**.

He ran **fast**.	He **quickly** shoveled the snow.	She typed the paper **perfectly**.
Sonja **carefully** turned the page.	Jason waited **patiently**.	We went to **Michael's** house.
It was a **good** movie.	Sherry made **delicious** cookies.	Karen had a **timid** cat.

He ate a **cold** sandwich.	Mom bought the **blue** plates.	The **fat** caterpillar crawled.
Mom asked me **politely**.	She swam **faster** than last time.	Mrs. Karls played **wonderfully**.
He colored the picture **neatly**.	Geralin picked the **yellow** flower.	She **sang** well last night.

In the Cafeteria (page 104)

1. today		7. after
2. next to		8. nearby
3. around		9. always
4. tomorrow		10. today
5. after		11. today
6. before		12. at home

Outer Space (page 105)

	Adverbs	Verbs		Adverbs	Verbs
1.	perfectly	placed	7.	brightly	shone
2.	slowly	rotates	8.	cautiously	climbed
3.	patiently	waited	9.	clearly	saw
4.	quietly	stared	10.	suddenly	noticed
5.	exactly	lined	11.	continuously	travel
6.	carefully	studied	12.	tightly	fastened

Letter of Complaint (page 106)

Dear Toy Company,

I bought a radio-controlled car last week. It's model number 2719. It doesn't work. We followed the directions, but we still can't get it to work right. We didn't make a mistake. My dad and I tried everything, but it just isn't working. When you push the lever to the right, it goes backward. It doesn't go forward at all. We can't figure it out. We're disappointed. We think it's defective. We hope you'll send us a new car. Our receipt is enclosed. We hope you'll honor our request.

Thank you,

Jared Jones

Our Soccer Team (page 107)

1. Robyn — She
2. Jason — He
3. team — We
4. Justin — He
5. The boys and girls — They
6. goalie — He or she
7. defenders — They
8. Sheila — She
9. girl — She
10. team — We or they
11. boys and girls — They or We
12. My dad — He

Pool Party (page 108)

It's	two	two	there
You're	It's	who's	It's
too	your	You're	to
you'll	There	It's	there

there	to	it's	whose
their	two	its	who's
they're	too		

The Garden Snail (page 109)

The following linking verbs should be circled:

| is | are | are | are | are |
| are | is | is | are | are |

The following action verbs should be underlined:

spends	comes	feeds	eat	eat
become	produce	move	gliding	
produce	lay	hibernates	live	

Car Wash (page 110)

Helping Verb	Main Verb
1. was	carrying
2. is	scrubbing
3. are	spraying
4. have	come
5. are	working
6. may	wash
7. is	filling
8. is	rinsing
9. is	getting
10. may	earn
11. is	spraying
12. was	having

Computer Fun (page 111)

1. I enjoy working on the computer, (but) sometimes I need to get up and stretch.
2. I like to play computer games, (and) sometimes I just like typing.
3. Everyone likes computer class, (but) it always seems to go by too fast.
4. Our computer teacher is nice, (but) sometimes he raises his voice if we don't listen.
5. Reba likes to work at the computer, (so) she does that during free choice time.
6. I work on the computer at school, (and) I use the computer encyclopedia at home.
7. We have a computer in our living room, (and) my Dad has one in the office.
8. Dad bought a digital camera, (and) he is learning how to load pictures onto the computer.
9. I like to take pictures, (but) I don't always hold the camera still enough.
10. Our camera is old and doesn't work well, (so) we bought a new digital camera.
11. We can store the pictures on a tiny disk, (or) Dad can put each picture inside the computer hard drive.
12. We took a family photo, (and) my mom printed it right at home.
13. Dad says the computer was a great invention, (but) the digital camera is an amazing machine.

Raccoons (page 112)

Verbs		Nouns	
survive	rinse	tent	frogs
eat	twist	raccoon	fruit
swims	fight	cooler	hands
catch	grows	cities	fingers
dip		face	coat
		fur	

Packer Football (page 113)

1. that	5. that	9. who
2. who	6. which	10. which
3. who	7. who	11. who
4. that	8. which	

Picnic (page 114)

1. real	5. very	9. real	13. very
2. very	6. very	10. very	14. real
3. very	7. real	11. very	15. very
4. very	8. very	12. very	16. real